KALEIDOSCOPE

NORTH LONDON

Edited by Dave Thomas

First published in Great Britain in 1999 by
POETRY NOW YOUNG WRITERS
Remus House, Coltsfoot Drive
Woodston
Peterborough, PE2 9JX
Telephone (01733) 890066

Copyright Contributors 1998

HB ISBN 0 75430 397 7
SB ISBN 0 75430 398 5

FOREWORD

This year, the Poetry Now Young Writers' Kaleidoscope competition proudly presents the best poetic contributions from over 32,000 up-and-coming writers nationwide.

Successful in continuing our aim of promoting writing and creativity in children, each regional anthology displays the inventive and original writing talents of 11-18 year old poets. Imaginative, thoughtful, often humorous, *Kaleidoscope North London* provides a captivating insight into the issues and opinions important to today's young generation.

The task of editing inevitably proved challenging, but was nevertheless enjoyable thanks to the quality of entries received. The thought, effort and hard work put into each poem impressed and inspired us all. We hope you are as pleased as we are with the final result and that you continue to enjoy *Kaleidoscope North London* for years to come.

CONTENTS

Ruby Begum   1
Joanna Caird   2

Acland Burghley School
    Mahad Ali   3
    Hannah Fair   4
    Oliver Probets   4
    Leon Farrell   5
    Sacha Coward   5
    Matthew Hesse   6
    Nichola Ioannou Vales   6
    Ayemere Oboh   7
    Tatiana Young   8
    Lance Oluyi   8
    Poorya Mehrmand   9
    Bode Alade   9
    Leon Elias   10
    Louis Dorman   10
    Lucy Hooker   11
    Roy Scott-Halcro   11
    Torquil Hopper   12
    Munir Eljaouhari   13
    Laura Case   14
    Sarah Humphrey   15
    Tim Russell   15
    Mpho Pule   16
    David Kennedy   16
    Tommy Paine   17
    Joanne Souster   17
    Samuel Gray   18
    Joe Hume   19

Belmont School
    Alexander Spencer-Todd   20

Channing School

Rowena Evans	21
Chantal Lust	22
Selina Lam	22
Maggie Bartrop	23
Bhavna Choraria	23
Nicky Allison	24
Kate Shorts	24
Sophie Hanina	25
Demetra Karacosta	25
Loba Behnia	26
Tamsin Shaw	27
Vanisha Patel	28
Judith Lee	28
Louisa Anderson	29
Zehra Harvey	30
Alexis Lyne	30
Rachel Elton	31
Emma McIlroy	31
Sorayya Shareef	32
Rachel Mackay	32
Jessica Levy	33
Helena Crow	34
Alice Shirley	35
Belou Charlaff	36
Emily Coates	37
Chloé Briggs	38
Emma Hatcher	38
Harriet Sharkey	39
Katie Elder	40
Samantha Fleming	41
Lydia Morton	41
Dina Grishin	42
Lara Mitchell	42
Clare Martin	43
Emilia Melville	44
Nina Nielsen-Dzumhur	45
Louise Smith	46

Erin Choa	46
Michelle Appleyard	47
Bahar Jalali	47
Amy Jones	48
Katie Badenoch	49
Sophie Hollender	50
Susannah Peel	51
Rosie Mitchell	51
Emma Mathews	52
Sophie Morelle	53
Coral Amiga	54
Florence Hogg	54
Elinor Hynes	55
Kimberley Pavyer	56
Anna Sharkey	56
Sophie Scott	57
Rachel Holloway	57
Jessica Pegram	58
Juliette Daigre	59
Laura Fitzpatrick	60
Paula Boulos	60
Hannah Lewis	61
Rosa Crawford	62
Amy Wilson Thomas	63
Catherine Pulford	64
Adele Harrison	65

Copthall School

Nimisha Vara	65
Lisa Durack	66
Sam Charalampous	67
Philippa Childs	67
Kerry McDowell	68
Joanne Selwood	68
Elena Pierides	69
Pooja Mahbubani	70
Zara Baker	71
Stella Constantinou	72

Kerry Quartly	73
Natasha Turner	74
Lauren Katy Vincelli	75

Edmonton County Lower School

Liam Woellhaf	75
Meha Mehta	76
Edmund Kirby	77
Deeya Balgobin	78
Angela Georgiou & Nicola Katsambis	79
Daniel Cutting	79
Rebecca Oyetey	80
Ruth Illsley	81
Stacey Hockley	82
Natalie Mott	83
Sinem Halil	84
Sophie Slater	85
Renan Hussein	86
David Weekes	87
Vanisha Mistry	88
Nadine Hart	89
Megan Hallsworth	90
Laura Mercer	91
David Priestley	92
Rebecca Emery	93
Hayley Stevens	93
Yiannis Panayi	94
Kai Shayler	94
Louisa Mali	95
Lydia Mousoullou	96
Samantha Wilson	97
Shelley Lodge	98
David McGhie	98
Sarah Small & Emily Yates	99
Melissa Bhikoo	99

Hendon School

Zoë Moss	100

Highbury Fields School

	Klara Brennan-Bernatt	101
	Catherine Louise Vitry	102
	Kelly Mills	103
	April Hodges	104
	Joanna McGavin	104
	Adeola Aderibigbe	105
	Soumaya Amrani	106
	Niamh Brennan-Bernatt	106
	Samantha Allen	107
	Donna Padfield	108
	Ayrun Nessa Begum	109
	Funda Civelek	110

Highgate School

	Fred Sorrell	110
	Ken Wee	111
	Sam Schneider	112

Hornsey School For Girls

	Nawel Belmouloud	113
	Monica Singha	113
	Veronica Hoggar	114
	Sara Stafford-Williams	115
	Lydia El-Aabdi	115
	Vidya Mohit	116
	Emily Dalton	116
	Mikhaila Fam	117
	Derya Yilmaz	118
	Layla Richardson	119
	Rehana Khatun	119
	Rajnin Ali	120
	Fiona Boateng	120
	Lottie J Hamer	121
	Hoi-Ling Li	121
	Sophia Awan	122
	Shamim Mussa	122
	Emma Gullick	123

Rosie Housman   124
Natalie Andrew   125
Dipa Uddin   126
Tamary Penlerick   127
Teisha Bradshaw   128

St James' Catholic High School, Colindale
Lauren Beary   129
Celia-Jane Ukwenya   130
Jason Cianfrone   131
Paul Doyle   131
Kieran Sexton   132
Lisa Swann   132
Daniel Hernon   133
Lee Kilcoyne   134
Messiac Chaminda James   134
Myles McEneny   135
Chris Mannion   136
Siobhan Munroe   136
Paul McFadden   137
Stephen Brady   138
Ciara Clifford   138
Timothy Meaney   139
Sharon Murphy   140
Ewan Gillies   141
Alexandra O'Neill   142
Lisa Maher   143
Emma Tuvera   144
Maireàd Conway   144
Dayo Olubodun   145
Christopher Coffey   145
Sara Daoud   146
Connie Abbe   147
Siobhan Hackett   148
Edel Gallagher   148
Jack Dennis Ryan   149
Tara Shanahan   150
Michelle Coyle   151

Daianne Cope   151
Stephanie Bohan   152
James Sealey   153
Gina Grandfield   154
John Michael Mullen   154
Francesca Donno   155
Coleen MacDonald   156
Clare Casey   157
Philip Morgan   158
Jenny Jackman   158
Elviae Casimir-Lascaris   159
Omar Henry   159
Laura Hunter   160
Alexandra Hazel   160
Neil Jahans   161
Lavinia Zecca   161
Stacey Hunter   162
Rachael Smith   162
Gary Casey   163
Leanne Kenny   164
Antonio Marcelino   164
Rory Leyne   165
Vincent Shailer-Dolan   166
Christina Fitzgerald   166
Joanne Mullins   167
Alice McGee   168
Declan McCarthy   168
Scott McNicholas   169
Jemma Barry   170
Rachel Slattery   170
Daniel Llewellyn   171
Kate Tracey   172

St Mary's CE High School, Hendon
Anneliese Clarke   173
Kyle Alveran   173
Louis Matccga   174
Ian Anoff   174

Chris McDonagh	175
Andreas Charalambous	176
Priya Makwana	177
Carmine Mattia	177
Michael Campbell	178
Forum Shah	179
Jahmai Turner	179
Tunde Hazzan	180
Velma Candy	180
Hagar-Iron	181
Shamaine Boyce	181
Karina Roseway	182
Carla Powell	182
Minal Wadhia	183
Nicole Bandoo	184
Jonathan Norton	184
Panish Patel	185
Sharon Yemoh	186
Akif Mehmet	186
Kieren Russell	187
Gabriel Gutierrez	187
Elakeche Ella	188
Lamarr Douglas	188
Neil Bennett	189
Daniela Holguin	189
Charitha Jayatilaka	190
Nicky Wong	190
Lavina Suthenthiran	191
Siân Saxton	191
Dilan Kanli	192
Manisha Sahni	193
Vanetta Richards-Lindo	193
Ramvir Singh Padam	194
Joanne Lindsay	194
Michelle Burgess	195
Janet Wong	196
Richard Coker	196
Susannah Sweetman	197

Reshma Patel   197
Catharine Bishop   198
Jermaine Raymond   199
Sadia Dhakam   200
Keith Clarke   200
Amanda Rashid   201
Julian Douglas   202
Robert Mitchell   202
Hitesh Kothari   203
Kate Marshall   203
Steven Gayle   204
Josephine Balfour   205
Shenalee Patel   205
Jessica Ward   206
Amir Pourdanay   206
Komal Patel   207
Aidan Nolan   207
Karl Martin   208
Kieran Wilkinson   208
Ricardo Reittie   209
Jason Case   209
Andrea Carr   210
Nelson Simon   211
Darren Zanre   211
Francine Leach   212
Patrick Edgcumbe   213

The Swaminarayan School
Alpa Patel   213
Hinal V Patel   214
Shirel Patel   214
Banshree Pindoria   215
Pooja Kanabar   216
Bhavin Patel   216
Rohini Patel   217
Ravi Ghodasara   217
Dharmesh Pankhania   218
Priya Kerai   218

Alopi Patel   219
Bina Tailor   220
Premvati Depala   221
Amar Mandavia   222
Jessel Savani   223

The Poems

MY SHOOTING STAR

Like a comet you will fly through the sky
so bright I will not even need to cry.
You will deliver your love and then shoot away
I will ask myself why
why all this?

Take me away like a shooting star
take me with you so afar.
Take me away from this world of pain
take me away before the rain.
My shooting star let the dream be and
open my eyes for me to see.
We will be together
two shooting stars
flying through the cloud, skies and the world.
We will conquer the skies
to deliver the stars below us,
we will pass the moon, and land there soon.
We will shoot through like the comet
          so discreet
we will pass the lunar eclipse
love will fall into darkness,
for my shooting star darkness will never fall upon,
only the light of the dusty stars above
will guide our light.
We have a mission to accomplish.
My shooting star.

Ruby Begum

CONCENTRATING BABE

The lips move in and out
The cheeks just gently up and down
Otherwise he is completely still
And completely silent
Except for the occasional contented murmur
Of the concentrating babe

His tears are forgotten
As he softly sucks
To the calming rhythm of her beating heart

She rocks him slowly to and fro
His quiet breath deepens in and out
The murmurs stop
His eyelids close
And as he begins to dream
He forgets he was hungry
And again she must remind him

The lips move in and out
The cheeks just gently . . .

Joanna Caird

SUMMER

Summer begins a new season
a new start, fresh flowers
hot sun, this is a special
new summer I will never forget.

People all around me
laughing and smiling
I wake up the next
morning, step out of my
house, put my sunglasses on
thinking of my day.

The sun beams down
on me as I sit on a
chair on the beach
I look up and see the
clouds closing in,
the day's dawning,
the day's gone.

There are only days,
weeks still left to
go, oh my summer.

Mahad Ali (12)
Acland Burghley School

SLEEPER

A lightweight toaster on my lap,
A silky hot water bottle full of fun.
Curled in a ball ready for a nap,
A ball that soon does succumb.

A small chest moves rhythmically up and down,
Tail twitching as dreams fill the mind.
Now thinking only thoughts of a sleeping clown,
Laying there in a timeless time.

In his heart and mind his dreams grow wilder,
And his feet begin to stir.
For he is now a sleeping tiger,
Who then begins to purr.

Hannah Fair (11)
Acland Burghley School

WATER

When water touches my lips
it feels soft like silk
it feels cool
relaxing and tranquil.
When the water travels
down my finger
it feels like a tidal wave.

Oliver Probets (12)
Acland Burghley School

TIME

Time for this,
time for that,
time for nothing,
I can't feed the cat.

Time kills,
time aids,
time makes history
and pictures fade.

Time makes you old,
and never young,
when you grow up
you can't have fun.

Leon Farrell (12)
Acland Burghley School

BED

Bed is a place to
relax and rest nice
and warm and
snuggled up far
away from any
thoughts of the
day slowly drifting
far away to the
beginnings of another
day . . .

Sacha Coward (11)
Acland Burghley School

DO MOUNTAINS EVER DREAM?

Do mountains ever dream
of the sea or the sand
dancing on the beach
where the ocean meets the land?

Do mountains ever dream
of river, lakes or seas
the laughter of the children
or the buzzing of the bees?

Do mountains ever dream
about eating iced buns
of reading Charles Dickens
or flying to the sun?

Do mountains ever dream
of walking on the moon
or meeting at a showdown
in a western at high noon?

Do mountains ever dream
of people tall or small?
In fact I've a question -
do mountains dream at all?

Matthew Hesse (12)
Acland Burghley School

WATER BED POEM

Water bed water bed sinking in.
Water bed water bed I've got a ring.

Water bed water bed in the night.
Water bed water bed you're so right.

Water bed water bed how do you do.
Water bed water bed how are you?

Water bed water bed I've had enough.
Water bed water bed it's just tough.

Nichola Ioannou Vales (11)
Acland Burghley School

SWEET TALK

I went to school, my lovely school
to see my friends
such friendly friends.
To see those teachers
the teachers I like
are the ones that are funny,
they give you jokes
and sometimes give you money.
But this is hardly ever,
for you have to sweet-talk them
and buy them flowers.
But even after that
they still say no
but take your flowers.
But some teachers are just so funny,
they keep you in stitches
and make you cry with laughter.
These are the teachers
I want to see in classes,
the ones that are in Acland Burghley,
the ones that are so cool.

Ayemere Oboh (12)
Acland Burghley School

THE FIGHT

Pulling hair, screaming hard
Beat! Beat!
You feel the heat
Bash! Bash! Smash! Ouch!
You tear and swear to win that fight!
You look at him and don't make a sound,
I don't want to hurt,
And everyone wins if they don't fight.
You may feel it tight,
But now I know . . .
       I'll never *fight!*

Tatiana Young (12)
Acland Burghley School

MOLE MAN

I think that I'll never see,
My cataracts are blinding me.

I think that I'll never hear,
My ears are clogged with
wax my dear.

I think that I'll never smell,
My nose was lost in the war.

I think that I'll never walk,
Thank heaven that I can talk.

Lance Oluyi (13)
Acland Burghley School

MY BALL

When I was young I found a ball
The ball was black, and I found it cool
It was the first ball I had of my own
So I took great care of it and played with it alone
No one ever saw it, not even my own parents
Until my friend came round, his name was Terrance
He saw the ball and said it was his
But I told him it belonged to my little cousin Liz
He didn't believe me by the look on my face
So I insulted him, and he gave me a chase
He caught me at last and gave me some digs
So I gave him the ball and we ate a few figs
He came to my house nearly every day
And we took the ball and went out to play.

Poorya Mehrmand (12)
Acland Burghley School

IS THIS THE END?

My mother told me one day it was gonna happen
But she never told me when
She told me it will happen when I was much older
Wish it would have happened then
Is this the end?
They were hitting us and whipping us for hours
In the hot baking sun
I never thought I'd live for another hour
But I did, thanks to God
Is this the end?

Bode Alade (12)
Acland Burghley School

IT'S CHRISTMAS TIME

John leapt up straight out of bed,
It's Christmas time, 'Hip hip hooray' he said.
He ran into his mum's room to wake her up,
He made her a cup of tea in her favourite cup.
He went into the living room to see the tree and present,
But what he saw wasn't too pleasant.
He ran upstairs to tell his mum,
'Someone's stole the tree and presents, come, come, come.'
'What presents?' asked his curious mum,
'The Christmas presents, God you're so dumb.'
His mum replied 'I'm sorry son, it's not Christmas today,
It's the 18th of June, Christmas is far, far away.'

Leon Elias (13)
Acland Burghley School

THE NEW SHORTER OXFORD ENGLISH DICTIONARY

The new *shorter* Oxford English Dictionary,
Well it could be true,
If you call 13cm thick, short,
Also the print is about 1½mm tall,
So the shorter English Dictionary,
Is not so short at all.
Those pocket ones too -
You'd have to have a big pocket.

Louis Dorman (11)
Acland Burghley School

THERE GOES THE GUN

Bang bang goes the gun
It hits you in the heart
With a big thump.

Your eyes feel heavy
Your body feels weak
That lump in your throat
Makes you want to choke.

That day has come
When you all wear black
And realize that they are
Not coming back.

Lucy Hooker (11)
Acland Burghley School

MY LEATHER JACKET

My leather jacket
is so soft and smooth
it feels as if
it is made for me
you see.

My leather jacket
is so rough and tough
it can go through anything
with me
you see.

Roy Scott-Halcro (11)
Acland Burghley School

AUTUMN

As the summer draws in
the nights seem closer.
When the leaves burn gold
and the animals go colder.

I sit in the corner
and dream of the future,
never knowing what will happen
in this time of hibernation.

I see a hedgehog starting to sleep,
eyes closing, spikes flapping,
heart resting as in yoga's
slow beat.

I see the conkers drop like parachutes
from the lazy moving sky.
Small children run
to find the largest one.

I see the conkers crash, smash,
to pierce each other's skin.
Children crowding round
whilst screaming out loud sounds.

Autumn is the time
filled with orange and brown.
Taking a break from excitement,
But not losing the comedy of the
clown.

Torquil Hopper (12)
Acland Burghley School

MY CAT

She's so cute
sitting on the floor
asleep - lifeless
not a movement.

But then she jumps
to life - ferociously
coming towards me
while I sit down helplessly
she's running like a maniac.

I still feel helpless
as she runs at me
then she jumps onto
my lap - and goes to sleep.

Again cute, lifeless
and not a movement,
she doesn't stir.

Munir Eljaouhari (12)
Acland Burghley School

KALEIDOSCOPE!

Life's spinning,
Falling in patterns.
It's a game,
Losing and winning.

Sometimes it's bad,
Terribly sad.
It's a tragedy.

But others . . .

It's happy,
And fun.
Life's just begun.

But . . .

Life's spinning,
Falling in patterns.
It's a game,
Losing and winning.

Laura Case (12)
Acland Burghley School

DOLPHINS

I was sad,
The dolphins came out.
My face was happy, happy at that.
I was like a dog fetching a stick.

I had to go.
I didn't want to.
I asked the man,
'Can I swim with them?'

The man said 'Yes,
You have to wear this wet suit,
They might bite!'

I thought they were beautiful.

Sarah Humphrey (11)
Acland Burghley School

CATS

Purring small lions, always on the
lookout for food.
Purring and miaowing. In the day hours
sleeping and waiting, in the night
on the prowl.
Those goggle emerald-green eyes open!
Running, jumping, leaping, eating.
Sitting in the sun, their tails wagging,
Their ears hearing, their noses sniffing.

Tim Russell (11)
Acland Burghley School

MY WEIRD FRIEND

I have a weird friend who
comes from outer space.
He lives in a cattle market
and has brown stuff on his face.
He has three legs and four arms
which are quite large,
when he comes to my house
he comes outside to play football with me.
My other friends call him 'flea-boy'
because he has a lot of fleas.
When he goes to visit his own world,
outer space,
before he goes I tell him
'Wash that brown stuff off your face.'

Mpho Pule (11)
Acland Burghley School

MY PENCIL CASE

My pencil case
is lovely to touch,
soothing, soft and cold.
It feels bumpy,
and relaxes me.
It makes me drift away.

David Kennedy (11)
Acland Burghley School

FOOTBALL

As I come out of the tunnel
I hear the roar,
it's even louder when I score.
One-nil, that's no big deal,
the fans want more to thrill.
The other team turn on the skill,
one-one now, I feel ill.
Five more minutes left to go,
and our team has won a throw.
From my head down to my toe,
I won't let this one go.
2-1, 2-1, the job is done,
the whistle blows and we have won.

Tommy Paine (11)
Acland Burghley School

SAND

As I walk along the sandy beach,
my feet slide through the smooth sand,
the cold air blows lightly against my face,
I can feel my feet sink into the sand,
As I pick up the tiny grains,
I feel them trickle down my hand.

Joanne Souster (12)
Acland Burghley School

THE JOURNEY

Engines throbbing,
Sirens wailing,
Horns honking,
People shouting.
I lie coiled like a spring
In my fast-moving bed,
While the sounds of the
City run through my head.

Bow doors clanging,
Boats swaying,
People sleeping,
People eating.
On top of the boat,
I look out to sea,
The salt-stinging wind
Pounding on me.

Campfire sparking,
Wolves howling,
Owls hooting,
Birds singing.
I'm sleeping in the tent,
Eating some food, thinking of
The journey and how it
Changed my mood.

Samuel Gray (12)
Acland Burghley School

THE FUNFAIR

The funfair is loud, with always
a crowd.
It is big and tall, but never
too small.
There are games and rides, with big
mat slides.
There are bumper cars, and aliens
from Mars.
I like the waltzers, they twist
and spin,
A world of dizziness, you are
in.
Look down at the lights, from the
big wheel's heights,
It's quite a fright.
I think I'm stuck, when I'm at the
top,
People start to rock,
rock.
The wind blows in my face,
it's quiet,
But down there, it's quite
a riot.
When I get down it's time
to go.

Joe Hume (11)
Acland Burghley School

JIMMY DAWN

He goes to school in the usual way,
His face looks like some modelling clay.
A trouble-maker is Jimmy Dawn,
Beady eyes and as thin as a prawn.

He never listens to the teacher,
He eats just like a filthy creature.
His fingernails are black with grime,
He is dreaming of a life of crime.

There is no one at home to cook his meals,
No one to ask him how he feels.
He sleeps in the corner by the bins,
Surrounded by bottles and empty tins.

His mum's new boyfriend treats him rough,
Jimmy never cries, he has to act tough.
His social worker knows the score,
But the boyfriend won't let her through the door.

Jimmy wants to rave and riot,
So they give him pills to keep him quiet.
All those girls with designer bags,
Won't look at Jimmy dressed in rags.

The social worker feels ashamed,
If things go wrong she'll get the blame.
But she's got cases just like Jim,
And there's nothing she can do for him.

At school they pray for children in need,
The children follow the master's lead.
'You should be grateful' the master adds,
'For good homes, loving mums and dads.'

And Jimmy gives praise for all this good,
But it's a world away from his own childhood.
So for children in need, they didn't ask to be born,
Who's looking out for Jimmy Dawn?

Alexander Spencer-Todd (12)
Belmont School

MY LOUNGE

A quiet room,
Warm and comfortable.
A place for relaxing,
A place for pastimes.

It is a room for amusement,
A place to set my spirit free.
Listening to my music and singing along,
Or happily improvising on the piano.

It is a family room,
A room for festivities and gatherings,
For special days and formal times.

A place for horseplay,
And for joking.
French doors open up to a
Wonderful garden full of colour.

This is a room special to me,
Where I hold most of my memories.
A place of calmness and joy,
A place to stand about in, and waste time.

Rowena Evans (12)
Channing School

THE CONTENTS OF MY HEAD

Within my mind
Beneath my skull
Dreams float
Untouched.

Within my dreams
Beneath reality
I think about
My own world.

Within that world
Beneath the pale blue sky
Hopes, dreams and ambitions
Take shape.

Within the thoughts
Beneath the hopes
Dreams become
Certainty.

Within my world
Beneath the sun
My life is
Perfect.

Chantal Lust (14)
Channing School

DEATH

Just what is death like?
I really do want to know.
So I'll try right now . . .

Selina Lam (12)
Channing School

BATHING

My favourite place is the bath;
It is unusually deep,
Like a steamy rock pool.

It has large fluffy bubbles,
like marshmallows,
that pop with pearlized colour,
and bob like icebergs.

The shampoos and conditioners are
lined up on the shelf
like a New York skyline,
and the coral like sponges
hang from the shower.

I love how the bath makes my legs feel like elongated corks;
all you can hear in the bath is the
leaf-like crackle of the bubbles as they burst.
You can smell warm water lingering
with an artificial strawberry bubble bath.
There is also a waft of soaps
coming from behind me.

Maggie Bartrop (12)
Channing School

THE VIOLIN

A brown body in a battered briefcase,
With f's for fingers, curly locks,
And a black backbone. Its vibrating voice
Sounds when horses' hairs slide over the smooth strands.
The tiniest of its kind, it makes the highest howl.

Bhavna Choraria (12)
Channing School

MY FAVOURITE PLACE

The smell of horses
mingles with a soft breeze,
and the sound of hooves clapping concrete,
and water buckets being topped.

A quiet atmosphere,
before a pony kicks its stable door
and picks at his hay,
as the day begins to wane.

And when I turn to leave,
my clothes are clogged with water and hay,
and my shoes are little oval mud-cakes.

Nicky Allison (12)
Channing School

AFTERNOON SUNLIGHT

A patch of the afternoon sun warms
Her velvet fur
She stretches contentedly as she
Falls on her side and yawns to show
Ivory teeth and sandpaper tongue.
Her purr is
Bee-like
Her pads are cushions for her killer claws;
Amber eyes complement her grey coat.
Now, the buzzing ball sleeps serenely
Under the smile of the dappled sun.
She is happy as long as she has
The afternoon sun on her velvet fur.

Kate Shorts (14)
Channing School

SILENCE

Pure, white sound
Stained and dripping wet,
Icicles of dark sweet red.
Silence all around and damp,
And then the unforgiving cramps.

Footprints in the trail of tears,
Each man struggling with tormented fears.
Juggling with guns and bags,
Circus-tent morals, begin to sag.

And once they sit within the mud,
Protected by the earth of blood,
The time draws near for the final shout,
They are heroes, is there doubt?

The ratta-tatta prayer begins to scream,
Piercing through the English dream,
For king and country they must love,
Repetitive prayers to those above.

Sophie Hanina (14)
Channing School

DEVIL

D readed devil
E vil eyes
V ile creature
I n charge of your mind
L ives its own terrible life.

Demetra Karacosta (13)
Channing School

PIECES OF A PUZZLE

A girl in her teens
Presents a cool demeanour.
This she contains and controls
In a family, *her* community, of warmth and love.

Ambition,
To be a vet.
Passions and interests,
The Arts and nature.

She reflects an accomplished arrangement of herself
Felt quite simple by others,
But they have not fully understood her,
Until the time is taken to recognise her properly.

Sitting underneath the blanket which is her face -
Is a package bursting with the images
She chooses to acknowledge,
Day after day.

The flight of a bird.

The pollution from cars in the High Street.

A puzzle represents her life,
Its pieces, the sectors of her life,
Past history, present events and future aspirations
Scattered randomly in a maze.

Her aim, to find them
As the days go by,
Always discovering and redefining herself more accurately
With each piece.

Her wish, to form a picture
On finding the last segment (of the puzzle),
That satisfies her,
Her definition.

Loba Behnia (14)
Channing School

THE HANDMADE BAG

The lace around it had begun to fray
Lifeless and isolated.
It seemed as if it was staring into space.
Some of the beads and intricate patterns had
begun to fall off, leaving small marked areas.
The smooth, light blue silk was crumpled
and in some areas had faded to brown.
A golden ribbon shone, lining the top.
It had been stitched by delicate hands
that had worked until early hours of the morning.
She had made it to impress and fool rich people
at fashionable parties.
Now, it sat on display in a glass cabinet
while interested eyes enquired about it.
When empty it was limp like dead,
but when full it bulged with promise.
She often filled it with expensive jewels,
gold watches, trinkets and bracelets.
Very soon it will decay altogether
leaving no trace of its whereabouts.

Tamsin Shaw (13)
Channing School

THE LIFE OF A SOLDIER

'Victory for Britain' they shouted joyously,
'I'll be back for Christmas' they told their wives.
'We'll be heroes when we get back, mate' they told each other.
But they were blind to the consequences ahead of them.

'Pack up your troubles in your old kit bag and smile, smile, smile!'
they sang wearily,
The troubles of the world bore down on their shoulders.
Smile, smile, that the war is nearly over but all your mates are dead.
But they were still blind to the consequences ahead of them.

'My mum, my wife, my family, I want to see them' they screamed
helplessly in pain.
They wailed and cried like children.
They gargled and rolled in pain, blood-soaked, slowly fading away.
Now dead, they had no consequences to face or future ahead.

Vanisha Patel (14)
Channing School

THE FINAL DEPARTURE

His face was gaunt
The skin sucked onto a bare skeleton
A mouth so thin, sunken in
A smile worn with the worry of time.
His eyes, lost in the depth of his sorrow
Hair limp, white, lifeless.
His spindly fingers like the legs of spiders
A bent body crippled with age
Spine shaped like the curve of a bow
Breathing hoarse, shallow, intermittent.
His body slips away
And silence falls as the breathing dies.

Judith Lee (14)
Channing School

IN THE TRENCHES

He slumps asleep; a sack of clay,
The stinging rain spears on.
Against the sandbags, limp and scarred
He lies - numb, drained and wan.

Although fatigue suspends his tears,
They seep into his dreams:
Ignored, kept hidden through the day,
In sleep, they burst strained seams.

These poisonous tears infect the night
And dreams gush in deep-stained:
Not merely flecked with thoughts of home
But drenched, engulfed, full-flamed.

He dreams of calm, of stillness, quiet,
Of apprehension crushed,
No spluttering guns to fill the gaps
Of choking men now hushed.

Of simple wants, like sleeping late
In soft, clean, lice-free sheets,
And hot baths - he indulges in
These once expected treats.

And plates piled high with meat and fruits,
The scent of fresh-cut hay,
And a bright-eyed girl, skin dappled with sun
Beside him under the may.

And so, each day drags on,
Each moment bleeds the fear:
The full-lunged screams of man and gun -
The yearning to be home, not here.

Louisa Anderson (14)
Channing School

WAIT, IT WILL SOON SUBSIDE?

Flocks of men crossing the bridge from sanity
Just over to the dark swamp of madness,
They are waiting, they know now what to expect.
When will they go west; when will their time come?
Anticipation, the helplessness,
Not their lips, not even their eyes will express
The torment, the loss, corrupting their minds.

In their sleep, visions, images crowd them;
Those past memories, future misfortunes
And the present knowledge, too consistent
No safety (shut those eyes): not even in sleep
Dreams substituted for darkness, no peace
Drown, sink, no solitude, nowhere to go.
What's left? Just misery, which won't subside.

Zehra Harvey (14)
Channing School

MY BAG

Everyone, look at my bag!
Prada, *soooo* expensive.
Look! Do look at my bag.
The sheer elegance
And cool designer simplicity.
Everyone, look. Look at my bag!
Black leather, soft and sleek
Lying on my shoulder.
Everyone, look. Do, do look at my bag!
The prime designer must-have
That is finally mine.
Everyone, look. Oh *do* look at my bag.

Alexis Lyne (14)
Channing School

FORGOTTEN?

A chilling scene surrounds their corpses.
In a far desolate corner, lost in the madness of war,
Two bodies lie face down, trodden into the icy ground.
Tangled in barbed wire and choking on the dirt and dust,
These two men took their last look at life.
So insignificant and forgotten they appear.
Yet miles away from this treacherous nightmare,
Families mourn for the death of their young boy.
If only they could see him now,
Hunched over his bayonet and smeared in dry blood.
Would they still believe that he died a proud death for his country?
The ground shudders as yet another pointless grenade is fired,
And the battle rages on, oblivious to these helpless soldiers,
Crumpled and battered into the muddy soil.

Rachel Elton (14)
Channing School

A GLISTEN IN THE SNOW

Every fleece of snow lay there,
Every snow web heavily loaded
With lumps of dense snow.
The waft of cool air breezes past the steeple trees
And whirls the leaves around.
They start to float gradually
Until they rest calmly
On the gloom of whiteness.
The stars above waltz
Around the luminous-toned moon.
Leaving twinkles of starlight to shadow across
The great pause of snow.

Emma McIlroy (13)
Channing School

IF ONLY I WERE ANYTHING

If only I were a butterfly
And could start anew in spring,
I'd have all the colours of the rainbow
Printed on each wing.

If only I were a fish,
And could freely swim all day,
I'd swim out to the ocean
And then swim back to bay.

If only I were a unicorn
The only one to live,
I'd be special and unique
And have so much to give.

If only I were anything
Except for what I am,
Then maybe I could stop pretending
That my life is so glam.

Sorayya Shareef (14)
Channing School

BLACKNESS

Blackness, surrounding,
Everywhere yet nowhere,
Unfriendly, empty.

No sound from within,
But the silence is noisy,
Breaking through blackness.

Rachel Mackay (13)
Channing School

THE PE BAG

In the cold confinement of the locker,
Feeling the walls closing in around,
The crisp aroma of dried earth,
Encrusted, layer upon layer on the bottom of hockey boots (far too
                                        small for the owner)
Like annual rings on a tree;
A compound of mud, from the weekly games in a water-logged field.
Light from the three hostile slits at the top of the locker,
Like the view-point of a gun barrel
Reflect against the unyielding form of the hockey stick
Cutting into the cotton material of the PE bag,
Sending films of colour and 'Slazenger' around the steely metal shell
                                        of the locker.

Twice a day, the distant murmur of young voices is heard
And a juvenile shadow turns a key in the lock, with a violent click;
Cascades of light, colours and sounds enter,
And a dirty, sticky hand reaches through the miasma that is beginning
                                        to spill out
And unhooks the white draw-string from its screw.

The pressed PE clothes are exchanged for hot school uniform.
Discarded in a corner of the gamy changing-room,
Kicked and trodden on,
The faded beige bag rapidly becomes brown and damp;
Only identifiable by the lazy green stitching of the initials in the
                                        right-hand corner.
The contents, ever decreasing as items are misplaced;
No longer the bulging bag of the term's beginning,
Now limp and lost,
Forgotten with a pile of unwanted garments on the changing room floor.

Jessica Levy (13)
Channing School

THE TWO GENERATIONS

Oh look at my fabulous bag, Gran!
They say that it's almost unique,
For it's exactly the kind of a bag, Gran,
That you need to join every cool clique.
It's dainty and dark, and it gleams like tin foil;
Its straps are so thin they don't show;
The clasp (which is gold) makes me feel almost royal,
And that label's designer, you know.

Why you really can't be very bright, child,
If you call that a bag, you have lied;
It looks like an earring to me, child,
And just what can you carry inside?
Not my useful fly-swat nor my rain hat,
Not my pliers nor denture-stick cream,
A bottle of gin could not fit into that,
Honestly, dear, it's obscene!

Now mine I would call a *real* bag, dear
And it's made from strong waterproof leather.
It may not be slimline and cool, dear,
But it feels just as light as a feather.
I can get in it much more than yours,
Like my shoe-horn and peppermint tin -
Yes, that black bag of yours, has so many flaws,
It should promptly be thrown in the bin!

Helena Crow (13)
Channing School

A BAG AND ITS BOY

Bang!
Down goes the bag to . . .
The corner.
The bottom of the box,
The place of the forgotten -
Or nearly forgotten.
The dear, faithful bag has gone in.
It will have to wait until it is needed.

Wait for what?
Another trip to a boring museum?
Another sleep-over party?
Another time when the schoolbag's strap breaks?

The schoolbag.
S*oooo* boring and black.
S*ooo* conservative.
So absolutely necessary.
Besides, the blue bag clashes with the uniform.

Then one dark night
The bag is grabbed.
Jerked from its crumpled palace.
Now it is stuffed full.
Bulging. Full of everything . . . anything.
Clock, clothes, food, money . . .
All squashed into one bag
Like sweets in a child's mouth.

The bag was hoisted onto the skinny shoulder
That shuddered with quiet sobs,
And off they went into the darkness.
A bag and its boy.

Alice Shirley (14)
Channing School

LESS THAN THIRTY LINES . . .

Less than thirty lines?
Oh heck.
Bother! That's two down the drain. Pain!
How can I possibly fit my whole life's experience
And wisdom into . . . ?
Drat! That's another two gone.
OK, This is it.
Her beautiful golden hair tossed wildly as . . .
No, I'll never fit that one in.
How about that one I wrote in Year Six?
The little brown mouse trembled in terror . . .
No, I'll never get in all that stuff about the train crash.
Maybe a haiku!
They're short.
The pink plum blossoms . . .
No, this is my last chance for fame,
Remember my name . . .
How about rhyming?
Her lovely face was pale
As she heard the ticking clock
She let out a ghastly wail,
But then . . .
Hmmm.
She had to rock? Tore her frock?
Maybe not.
How many lines is this?
Twenty six!
Only four left.
I've said nothing! Nothing!
Oh, I've got it!
Wait, I just wanted to say . . .

Belou Charlaff (13)
Channing School

THE FAT KID

He climbs the bell tower steps,
His sweaty hands gripping the metal banister,
His oddly shaped feet stumbling.
Twice he hesitates -
Wonders if it is the right thing -
But he knows there is no alternative.
It has gone too far.
He reaches the top,
And now he is wracked with sobs,
Tears of hatred and relief
Dripping off his double chin
Onto his oversized belly.
He drops his bag onto the cold stone floor
And pulls out a thick, coarse rope.
He ties this to the ceiling, and makes a noose,
Then, standing on a chair,
He puts his head through the loop.
He whispers goodbye to all those who never cared
And jumps.
He does not scream.
His bullies find him
Hanging there
And they throw things at the body,
Laughing,
Not caring -
He was just a fat kid.
And the parents say nothing of it.
They don't feel the need to.
These are only children:
They don't mean badly.

Emily Coates (12)
Channing School

OH THE SLOANES

She enters the boutique,
Swung across one shoulder,
immense wealth drips.
The bag signifies her class,
        Upper.
Heads turn as she taps
across the floor.
Assistants natter among themselves,
classy, elegant words dropped.
This bag can intimidate you
and put you in your place.
This one accessory is the statement.
One label on its side.

Chloé Briggs (14)
Channing School

UNTITLED

Red faced, two eyes peeping
Black hat, permanent smile
Predator-like, eyeing his prey
He sits in silence . . .

Dawn breaks, up and ready
Stands still to attention
Violently thrust heavenward
Flying to his task . . .

Back and forth, tugged relentless
Inhales the grime through his trunk
From room to room - never ending
My . . Faithful . . . Henry . . .

Emma Hatcher (14)
Channing School

USELESSNESS

Alone
the bag sits
stranded on the street corner.
Full of things nobody wants,
heavy bottles wear holes in the bottom.
Chewing gum stuck to the inside
acts like blue tack.
Holding on to whatever touches it.

As the lonesome bag
sits marooned on the corner.
It dreams of past days
when it too was useful.
Days of gleaming bright lights
surrounded by food.
Days when it was accompanied by other bags.
He remembers the excitement each morning,
each bag hoping it would be their turn
to do their duty.

None of the young eager bags
would ever guess the fate they could endure . . .

Harriet Sharkey (14)
Channing School

CHINESE WHISPERS

We sat in a circle, deadly silent.
Everyone of us with smiles on our faces.
Denying all knowledge of cruelty and excitement.

She started it off.
It was at least a minute before she had finished.
A wicked smile came over the first person.
I will never forget it!

Quicker and quicker it spread.
Like a rash, everyone catching it.
It had stamina.

Nearly my turn now!
Spreading rapidly, it ate everyone,
People were talking immediately.
I felt a shiver down my spine.

Two more people, that's all it would take.
As it consumed the last person, enjoying every bit,
My head felt like it would burst with curiosity.

She leaned over.
It came flooding into my ear.
My eyes opened wider
As the plague took over me.

Now the world whispers that disease.
Every corner I turn,
It is there lurking - waiting.
It slowly eats away at me,
Every day - since then!

Katie Elder (12)
Channing School

GOSSIPING

Mum's friends come to tea,
What do they do?
They gossip!
They go:
Yak, yak, yak!
Quack, quack, quack!
Chit, chat, yak, yak!
Tongues flying
Fast, fast, fast!
'Did you hear? I know!'
'You'll never guess what she did yesterday!'
All night, all day, all week, all month, all year!
Never stopping
Always different
Gossiping . . . every time they meet!

Samantha Fleming (13)
Channing School

JUST A FEW SPITEFUL WORDS . . .

Just a few spiteful words,
slither across a line of eager forked tongues.
It grows large as it devours more hateful lies.
Surging - ever growing like the sea.
Treacherous, like its waves, as they engulf you.
An endless torment of lies.
And you are caught up in a web of deceit.
Building like a tornado and destroying everything in its wake.
A crawling serpent growing larger and larger.
Until it strangles you.
All this hurt comes from
just a few spiteful words!

Lydia Morton (12)
Channing School

INTERVIEW WITH A FEATHER!

'Tell us Mike! What's freedom like?'
Different for everyone, but for me . . .
It's like an always open door.
A Motorway without speed limits.
An everlasting funfair ride.
A trip to blissful heaven.
And without it?
Without it I'm like . . .
A fish without its sea
A bee without its honey
A harp without its strings
A businessman without money.
What do you do when you're free?
When free . . .
I fly above the clouds
I visit famous places
I gallop with the horses
I travel with the rainbow
I float with the snowflakes
And smile to the world!

Dina Grishin (13)
Channing School

CAT!

Creeping stealthily along the brick wall.
Glancing sideways, careful not to fall.
Her sleek black fur shimmers in the moonlight.
Her long sharp claws clutching the wall tight.
Her emerald eyes, glaring at her prey.
One quick pounce and let's call it a day . . .

Lara Mitchell (12)
Channing School

DRAGONFLY

Electricity runs like a river
Through the body
Multi-coloured neon from
Green to turquoise to blue.
The wings glistening and shining
Like the shimmer of
Light on ice
As delicate as a sheet
Of silver leaf.
A brightly-coloured totem-pole
A moving streak of
Electric blue lightning.

Delicately landing for
Merely a second.
The bullrush barely bends.
Once again it's off, never
Resting. Darting and
Dancing in and out of the sunbeams.

The reflection on the
Pond cannot match
The beauty of
The insect in flight.

Clare Martin (12)
Channing School

MAKING MOUNTAINS OUT OF MOLEHILLS

Lurking around corners,
waiting to snatch up and spread the news like wild fire.
Even the tiniest molehill is blown up to the size of Mount Everest.

'Why? Where? When? And who with?'
voices whisper,
stopping short as I approach,
babbling on when I have passed by,
filling their ever growing appetite.

'Why? Where? When? And who with?'
eyes ask,
peering incessantly from behind curtains,
darting away as soon as they are seen.

'Why? Where? When? And who with?'
Like distant mountains,
the nearer I get,
the further the voices seem,
until they are caught off guard and are as loud as a stormy sea,
crashing at the foundations of the very mountains they are creating.

Emilia Melville (12)
Channing School

CHINESE WHISPERS

A strong gale
spinning round threatened words.
Rearranging the innocent meanings
and violently in disgust, spitting them out.

Guess what!
Have you heard?
Did you know?
Oh! I know!

A hungry fire
persistently burning whispers.
Thick black smoke
a ravenous scavenger!

Guess what!
Have you heard?
Did you know?
Oh! I know!

A glistening snowball of words
gathering extra letters of consequence.
Crashed down exploding damaging messages.

Guess what!
Have you heard?
Did you know?
Oh! I know!

Nina Nielsen-Dzumhur (13)
Channing School

REVEALING SECRETS!

It spreads like wild fire
Across the plains of self confidence.
From ear to ear it grows
Expanding with every word.

Secrets revealed
Pull the trigger
And from that moment
Social death strikes
Persistently devouring dignity and pride
Wherever it descends.

Vicious circles of gossip create guilt.
Guilty gossip.
Undeniable consequences of
Revealing secrets!

Louise Smith (12)
Channing School

THE DRAGON OF THE CANDLE

The flame is burned from the candle
Light is no more.
Darkness enveloped, wreathed with swirls
Of silent smoke.
Swirling, ghosts of soft mist
Like a dragon of a candle.
Unfurling its splendour,
Climbing elegantly towards the sky
Of empty nothingness.
Until it puffs drifting into a clouded mist
And slowly floats and vanishes.

Erin Choa (11)
Channing School

CHIPPY

Soft silky satin ears
Stand straight like Meercats.
Thin white whiskers
Twitching in the breeze.
Deep brown eyes
Glisten like sunlight.
Small damp nose
Smells millions of miles away.
Long wet tongue
Laps water loudly.
His sandy brown and white coat
Soft as can be.
Short stumpy tail
Wags when happy . . .

Michelle Appleyard (11)
Channing School

THE EAGLE

They swoop swiftly down
with a hungry look in their eyes
they gaze at their prey.

With claws ready to pounce
under their big feathered wings
they step forward
In an instant, they violently hurt their prey.

After they have dined
they graciously fly away
Not feeling any guilt whatsoever
Gone . . . !

Bahar Jalali (11)
Channing School

LION OR MOUSE?

Me, I'm Amy
short name, short person.
I'm loud but quiet,
I'm kind but stubborn.

But I live two lives
I am two people!

At school I'm timid
as shy as a mouse.
The class are all cats
so I hide in my shelter.

At home I'm loud
I act like a lion.
King of my territory
prowling my jungle.

But I live two lives
I am two people!

At school I'm short
I'm shy, I'm scared.
At home I'm colossal
I'm clamorous, I'm captain.

But I live two lives
I am two people!

I dread the morning
the journey to school.
A day of hiding
of not being me.

Living one life
The life that I fear.

On the way home, the decibels rise.
The lion returns.
The inner me breaks free
And not a moment too soon . . . !

Amy Jones (14)
Channing School

THE LUXURIOUS MAMMAL

The thin sleek cat
Walking with stealthy footsteps.
Her head up high - in a proud fashion
And her tail trailing elegantly alongside her feet.
The cat's thin, dry tongue
Fondles with her clammy wet nose.
As she proceeds to lick it.
Her luscious green eyes turn to me
As she meows, making it clear that she is cold
As she begins to shiver.
Her delicate, thin wiry whiskers start to vibrate.
She jumps onto my lap using her light agile legs.
Curls up in between my knees and settles down to sleep.
I stroke her long wispy tail
As she entwines it around my wrist
In an effort to distract me.
Suddenly . . .
With one large leap she jumps off my lap onto the floor.
As I turn I see her luxurious tail
And small immaculate paws disappear
And she leaves my room . . .

Katie Badenoch (12)
Channing School

MAGPIES

After stealing and pinching
all day long.
The magpie's stomachs growls.
So when they've washed
their black and white plume,
they come to eat . . .

Their sleek and shiny beaks
prod and peck the ground.
Looking for delicious worms
to eat for their supper.

Slowly they move about
on the lawn.
Too intent on their business
to notice the world around them.

And when they have eaten
to their heart's content.
They spread out their
coal black wings
and fly away . . . !

Sophie Hollender (11)
Channing School

THE WAITING HOUND

There he faces out to sea
Over a cliff edge, watching me.
There he watches, there he waits
'Till invisible hands touch invisible gates.
He waits for his master to come back from the sky
And open those gates, to show he didn't die.
There he sits still, he just sits and waits
'Till invisible hands touch invisible gates.

Every evening he sits and he howls
Mourning distress to the moon.
Though his master's not come yet.
The hound's sure he'll come soon.
Memories haunt the waiting hound
Sitting all alone . . .
He remembers that awful day
Shaking to the bone . . .

Susannah Peel (11)
Channing School

LOVE

Love is a friend, not an enemy
It can be felt and not seen.
It can grip you in ecstasy
Then plunge you into the unknown.
Love can conquer all feelings
It can steal your very heart.
Then shatter it into fragments
Destroying your very soul.

Rosie Mitchell (13)
Channing School

A SUMMER POND

The pond was surrounded
by a mass of emerald green bullrushes,
with their vertical, oblong brown soft ends
swaying in the breeze.
The sun was shining on the water
making it dazzle and shine.
There was a fair wind
gently ripping the water and
from one bullrush to another
a spider was building his web,
using a swaying method
to reach the other bullrush.
Suddenly, a toad with a brown-green warty back
jumped from the pond
and landed on one of the many lily pads,
dotted randomly about the pond.
A speckled newt, climbed steadily out of the pond
to lie on a brick and bask in the warm sunlight.
A pondskater slid along the surface.
The frog's eye twinkled
and in a split second
the pondskater was gone!

Emma Mathews (11)
Channing School

THE FOX

Two bright eyes glare at me
as I walk towards the young fox.
His long matted tail
twitches - as if in debate.
His front paw lifts in anticipation.
Waiting and watching . . .
He wonders when this beast
will jerk forward!
Arms outstretched
to grab this fearful flesh-denied fox.
Bright eyes still glare.
Unblinking . . .
As I edge my way forward.
In his incessant glare I can see
fear of the beast on two legs.
His ears twitch
Nervously . . .
Cautiously - I edge forward.
Suddenly one paw drops down, closely followed
by the other paws.
Sudden speed . . .
Across the icy tarmac
Away from me . . .
Taking his glare with him!

Sophie Morelle (11)
Channing School

MY PLACE . . .

I swiftly walked down the twisted bendy road.
The mellow trees swayed from side to side
And I heard a whisper beyond the sweet air.
The sparkling river flowed.
A black blanket stretched across the sky.
With little lights scattered all over
Where was I going . . . !
I didn't know at all.
I just knew I was going to my place.
Where everything would be all right.
Somewhere far away.
The snow lay everywhere upon me.
I could hear it crunching, beneath me
A faint sweet smell emerged.
I was nearly there . . .
A few more paces . . .
And there would be my destiny;
I finally reached it
My place . . . my special place!

Coral Amiga (11)
Channing Schoo

WINTER

The cool wind caresses my cheek.
The virgin snow seems to crunch under my shoes.
My face burns with a delicious sensation of coldness
My eyes sting and water - as the wind hits my face.
I feel a delectable sensation of joy and merriment.
For it's my favourite time of year . . . winter!

Florence Hogg (13)
Channing School

TEEN ANGST!

I love to think deeply
I wish I was deeper!
Only a teenager
Wishing for harmony
Wishing for attention.
Often confused, lost thoughts
Sad thoughts, never clever
And seldom deep thoughts.
Imagining other creatures
Imaging another wilderness.
Thinking of lost ones
Seeking their spirits.
Thinking of all true meanings
Listening to deep songs.
Still only a lonely teenager
Straining for deepness
Straining for attention.
This and that still confusing
Here and there ever lonely.
Little mistakes, little problems
But big worries!
Carry sad thoughts
Continuing to make
Teen angst . . . !

Elinor Hynes (14)
Channing School

STARS AND RAINDROPS

Love, like stars in a night sky,
Each one glitters with a happy memory.

Love is like raindrops falling from clouds,
A single thought reflexes in their shapes.

A pool of glimmering water
The reminder of that love.

Stars return every night
So you never forget their sparkle.

The pool dries up into clouds
So rain may fall again . . . !

Kimberley Pavyer (14)
Channing School

GUILT

He sits at my side.
My only friend.
He forms my feelings
Moulds my secrets.

He accompanies my sleep.
My devoted guardian.
He watches my dreams,
Hears my thoughts.

He is always with me.
My silent companion.
Eating away inside me
Feasting throughout the years.

Anna Sharkey (14)
Channing School

UNCONDITIONAL LOVE

Look into my eyes
Show me who I am.
Let me see my heritage
My past, my potential.
Hold steadfast
Shower me with love
That knows no bounds.
Mother, give me acceptance
For everything I am
Show me I exist.
And that all the love I need is inside.
Father, when I'm wrong,
Don't punish me, but explain
To me where I fell
And make me aware of those I've hurt in the process.

Sophie Scott (13)
Channing School

MIST . . .

Hangs in the air
Like an unidentified presence
Drifts noiselessly
Seemingly motionless
Light water vapour rises up from the ground
Unseen at close range . . .

Rachel Holloway (13)
Channing School

THE LAST TREE IN THE FOREST

She stands alone
In the crusty earth.
The final tree in the forest
Her last leaf.
Shrivelled and brown
Swaying in the air.
As it falls to the ground.
The wind whistles
Through her brittle branches.
Her swollen trunk
Deserted by its past inhabitants,
Moans in the midday heat.
The sun burns into
Her aching structure.
Stiffening the heavy air.
She stands alone
In the crusty earth.
The final tree in the forest!

Jessica Pegram (13)
Channing School

HUNTER

Frog
Sits on the lily-pad *waiting!*
His beady eyes scan the area
Searching for a fly
That may happen to come along.

Waiting all day
Still as stone
Not one thing to give him away
But the flickering of hunger in his eyes.

At last, a movement in the air
Long thin tongue snakes out
Darts . . .
Quickly recoils towards his mouth
A short, easy action!

Suddenly his face contorts in pain and disgust
He writhes on the lily-pad
Spits out the creature
Wasp continues his journey
Unharmed . . . !

Juliette Daigre (13)
Channing School

THE SQUIRREL'S SECRET

The squirrel steps onto the fence
Its eyes darting around to see if anyone is
dangerously near.
His ears flicker backwards and forwards to
hear even miniature sounds.
Running along the fence using his big bushy tail
for balance he finally stops.
In one clawed hand he holds a nut.
Using his senses he looks around warily
while he darts toward the plants in pots.
Freezing yet again, he sees if anyone is coming.
He starts to dig ferociously, deep into the
soil, then leaves the nut there for safety
and puts the soil back neatly.
He darts away into the fresh morning air
hoping nobody knows his secret.

Laura Fitzpatrick (11)
Channing School

THE JEALOUS CHILD

She's always been better than me
In every way!
Everyone prefers her
She's prettier and a straight 'A' student
Why can't I be like her?

Everyone looks up to her
Respects her.
I'm treated like a failure.
Like nothing - someone from a lower class.
I could be just as good as her
Well maybe not as pretty or clever!
She's a perfect child
Why can't I be like her . . . ?

Paula Boulos (13)
Channing School

THE HUNTER

His gleaming green eyes gaze upwards.
Claws come slowly from sheaths.
The sunshine shimmers down
Onto his arched, black back.
Like a tiger he prepares to leap
Daggers scrape down the fence
As he hauls himself up.

The feather flutters on the fence.
Watchful, he creeps forward.
Tail erect for balance
His green eyes eager and excited.
In a flash he pounces.
Feather protruding from mouth,
He carefully clambers down . . .

Hannah Lewis (11)
Channing School

I HATE SAMANTHA FROM HULL

'Just phone this number and the CDs could be yours!'
Says the presenter, grinning.
I grasp the phone
I dial the competition line
My palm's perspiring
As I tell the computerised voice
My name
My mind races
As I repeat my address
And post-code.
I return to watch the television
To see if I have won
Those coveted CDs
'And the winner is . . .'
For a moment I think I've won;
I image the presenter's voice
'The winner is Rosa Crawford from London.'
The euphoria
The CDs
All mine . . .
But as usual, it was not meant to be -
'And the winner is . . . '
I hate Samantha from Hull.

Rosa Crawford (13)
Channing School

TEENAGERS ARE TROUBLE!
A PARENT SPEAKS . . .

I've got a lot to say
But I haven't got all day
Put in a very simple way
Teenagers are trouble!

Always late for every outing,
Flicking hair and pouting
Slamming doors and shouting
Teenagers are trouble!

When will she wake up?
There's more to life than make-up.
She longs for school to break-up
Teenagers are trouble

But despite my consternation
Sleepless nights and aggravation
I wouldn't trade her for anyone
Teenagers are fun!

Amy Wilson Thomas
Channing School

JETHRO

He sits on the gatepost
And basks in the sunshine.
People stroll past and stroke him
He purrs, rubs up against them
No one comes
So he limps inside
To curl up by the fireside
And remember the days
When he was young . . .

He used to be a hunter, a tiger, a beast.
His forefathers used to feast on the remains
Of animals from the African plains
And Jethro would also . . .
The mice of the house used to fear every night
Every night several went missing
Never to be seen again
And every mouse wondered
When it would be their turn . . .

Now he just lies there
And remembers those days
When he was young
When?
A long time ago . . .

Catherine Pulford (11)
Channing School

FOOD CHAIN

Sliding along so slowly
The slimy body slithers
With a wiggly, jiggly print
Crossing the massive patio
At zero point zero
Miles per hour.
Aiming for the delicious lettuce
Crawling over broken branches
With amazing acrobatics
Every ten seconds
A look around
Deadly danger near
Will the shell protect him?
From the bird's powerful sword . . . !

Adele Harrison (11)
Channing School

BIG BIG PAIN . . .

My name is Jane
I'm a big big pain
and I hate the rain.
So then I travel by train.
That's a big big pain
When we have friends around.
We watch Homeward Bound
and that's a big big pain . . .

Nimisha Vara (13)
Copthall School

MY DAD IS PEACEFULLY IN HEAVEN!

I got home from school and put on the TV.
I watched whatever was on.
My mum was cooking dinner
My dad was at work
and I was eating strawberries and cream.

There was someone at the door
The Police rang the bell.
My dad had been taken ill
I was in my room
My mum was crying
and my sister was in the loo.

They had to go to hospital
on blue lights
Rushing through cones
and red lights.
My dad was in intensive care
My mum was with him
and I was crying in bed.

My dad died three days later
He was in a coma and could
not speak.
I was holding his hand
My mum was crying
and my dad was peacefully in heaven . . .

Lisa Durack (13)
Copthall School

MY ONE NIGHT LOVER

Did my heart love till now?
For swear its sight.
For I never saw true beauty
till this night.

I gave you my love in vain.
My body never knew such pleasure.
But my heart never felt such pain.

Even if you took my heart
and tore it apart.
I would love you still forever and a day.
Never will my love go away.

Till death do us part . . . !

Sam Charalampous (13)
Copthall School

THE BABBLING BROOK

The babbling brook bounced
joyfully over the boulders.
The river rushed by like
it was running to win a race.

The stream swerves and swivels
the water washes wet rocks.
While it wastes its time waiting.

The silent lagoon lays lazily
with its logs under the sun
throughout the long lasting day.

Philippa Childs (13)
Copthall School

HALLOWE'EN!

It's Hallowe'en today - all the kids
come out to play.

It's Hallowe'en tonight - it will give
you such a fright.

Little Janey Bevil turned into a devil
and frightened the Mummy away.

Her Mummy came back from the dead
while little Janey was in bed.

She got out of bed
then fell down the stairs
and went straight back to bed
and then dropped down . . . dead!

Kerry McDowell (13)
Copthall School

SISTERS!

Sisters! Sisters!
They're always having fights.
Sisters! Sisters!
Should know each others rights.
They're always getting into trouble
Because they're bad when as a double.

Sisters! Sisters!
Will never get along
One will blame the other
For doing something wrong.
Sometimes sisters are the same
And sometimes they are not.
But my sister is just like me
Yet she annoys me quite a lot!

Joanne Selwood (13)
Copthall School

FOOTBALL!

Football is my hobby
Football all year round
Football on the ground
Football in the evening
Football is a great feeling
Football is a ball
Football with a ball
Football at school
Football in the hall
Football at the park
Football in the dark
Football as a team
Football in a dream
Football is my hobby . . .

Elena Pierides (13)
Copthall School

WALKING IN A DREAM

Walking through the cold, scary graveyard.
With the crunching and crumbling of the
leaves and twigs under my feet.
The wind was singing her first tune of
the long night ahead.
Owls were howling away while the
thunder and lightning went on and on.

It was like walking in a dream
but it was so real.
It was like my whole life flashed by
like a bolt of lightning.
It was like I was walking to the
edge of the world and everything was
just slipping out of my fingers and
vanishing with the crashes of thunder.

Then I awoke and the scary, cold graveyard
with the crunching and crumbling leaves
and twigs were gone.
The wind singing,
The owls howling - could be heard no more.
The thunder and lightning had disappeared.

My feelings have gone astray
My dream has vanished . . .

Pooja Mahbubani (13)
Copthall School

IT'S A DOG'S DINNER!

I am hungry, what can I eat?
I need something very sweet!
Sweet and sour greyhound, sounds very nice,
but I actually fancy
something with rice!
Labrador curry, I might die! Why not bull terrier pie?
Battersea Dogs Home, the local take-away,
Shall I order Jack Russell and chips - with extra mayonnaise!
Sounds very tasty - it may seem
but I'm actually not that keen!
I'm going to have
Poodle Kebabs!
I've finally decided what to eat,
but I might just have some Shredded Wheat . . . !

Zara Baker (13)
Copthall School

LIFE ITSELF . . .

In all my life
I've never known
the true fact
that I'm all alone
but life goes on
forever more.
So tell me my love
that I'm all yours
the good things and bad.
We have to face facts.
So let it be
that we're all
sometimes in love.
The ones that say
though deep inside
with laughter and happiness
all the way.
They're the ones
that truly know
deep inside
that they're all alone . . . !

Stella Constantinou
Copthall School

STORMY NIGHT

As I lie in bed
I can hear the rain
Going pitter patter on the window pane.

I can hear the rustling of the leaves
as the wind is blowing
through the trees.

All of a sudden I jumped with fright,
There was an almighty bang
On this dreadful night.

I hear a dog bark
And a cat makes a screech.
How I would like to be
on a sunny beach!

The door I hear creaks
and as it opens - I peer
It's only mum . . . she says
'Are you all right, dear!'

Kerry Quartly (13)
Copthall School

FACES AT WAR

Smiles upon their faces
Lining up to fight.
They think that it is all a game
A game of fun and delight.

Smiles upon their faces
Happy and full of glee.
Unaware of what approaches
Or how wicked it will be!

Frowns upon their faces
The dirt and smelly trench.
The crowded area and filthy clothes
And the wild, wicked stench.

Fear upon their faces
As the guns begin to blow.
Blood and pain are tightly bound
Around this fearful show.

Pain upon their faces
As explosives start to kill.
Animosity takes over
The bucket of death begins to fill.

Nothing upon their faces
They join the sea of death.
It was not a war of hope and love
But a war of pain, fear and death . . .

Natasha Turner (14)
Copthall School

LOVE!

When you love someone
You can't stop loving them.
Your mind thinks of nothing else but them.
When you love someone
You want them to love you too.
You don't want to be treated like a fool.
If you wed that person you love
You would want a bed
With two white doves at the end.
Doves are a symbol of friendship and love.
And when they are flying
You look above
Higher and higher and away they fly.
You don't want to say goodbye
When they leave you - you can't help but cry . . .

Lauren Katy Vincelli (13)
Copthall School

LIFE

Life
What is it all about?
Why do we run around, scream and shout?
Why do we work away, slaves to big men in high places?
Why do we do these things we complain about so often?
Why don't we have fun all the time?
Why do we do the things we do?
Why can't I do what I want to do?
I want to do things with him and with you
Why can't I do what I want to do?

Liam Woellhaf (13)
Edmonton County Lower School

THE SHIP OF DREAMS

Beyond the murky waters on the bed of the sea
A graveyard sits.
The Ship of Dreams, the Unsinkable
Lies at the bottom of the Atlantic.

Close your eyes, imagine
Think of all the lost lives
Think of loved ones
Clasping each other's icy hands
Pushed apart by a panicked crowd.

Think of one half on a lifeboat
Staring through her tears at her other half on the ship
And her warm, salty tears
Mingling with the icy Atlantic.

Think of the cry 'Women and children first,'
Think of the pain as this stabs through young lovers' hearts.

Think of the laughter heard before this dreaded iceberg appeared
And brought fear and terror to innocent people.

But look, see how quickly sadness has arrived
Only the fittest will survive
As the Titanic meets her death
And the death of lives, hopes and dreams.

Her eyes search the other lifeboats
Wondering, praying, hoping that he's there
But not seeing his smiling face.

The only person interested in her ambitions, dreams and goals,
Snatched away,
By man's ignorance thinking he could control nature.
Her loss and anger, shamed with others,
Felt for the rest of their lives
All wondering if there's any point in carrying on
After this Ship of Dreams was soon flooded with nightmares.

Meha Mehta (14)
Edmonton County Lower School

SAM THE SPACE AGE HERO

Sam the Space Age hero saved the galaxy each day:
He killed the evil Simiyads with one swipe of his shining ray.
This really helped to keep the Simiyads at bay.
All the people in the galaxy said, 'Sam, make those Simiyads pay.'

One day Sam saw a Simiyad sailing by a star
The Simiyad saw him and shouted, 'Ha, ha!'
This made Sam smile and he grasped a big crossbar.
The Simiyad saw this and he shuddered at the thought
Of a crossbar landing on his throat.

He quickly turned his ship around and sped far from the place.
Sam quickly chased him into the depths of space.
The Simiyad's ship began to slow and the Simiyad's face grew grim.
After all there are not many petrol stations out there on
                                        the galaxy's rim.

Sam's smile shone and he snatched his shining ray.
He fired it at the Simiyad and it fried him right away.
So Sam the Space Age hero saved another day.
With his shining ray and his speeding ship
He will put the Simiyads away.

Edmund Kirby (13)
Edmonton County Lower School

AN INDESCRIBABLE FEELING

'It's indescribable,'
She said
But I never understood it
Now I know what she meant

It's indescribable
Only when we experience it
We realise
That words cannot express it

It's indescribable
Whatever the language
We cannot find
A good explanation

It's indescribable
I cannot say what it is
Happy? Sad? Magic?
No, these are just shallow words

It's indescribable
Feel it, live it
And you will see
That it's only 'indescribable'.

Deeya Balgobin (13)
Edmonton County Lower School

YOUNG LOVE

Yesterday I saw your face,
then my heart began to race.
I love to look into your eyes,
they shine like diamonds in the skies.

I wonder what you think of me,
looking at you, can you see?
I'm always dreaming about you,
I wish you would dream about me too.

I can't help feeling this way,
seeing you every day.
I feel dreamy, oh so small,
seeing you walking down the hall.

I really hate feeling this way,
to your face I just can't say.
Your hair it shines just like the sun,
for me I think you're the only one.

Angela Georgiou (13) & Nicola Katsambis (14)
Edmonton County Lower School

THE SOLDIER

His eyes are like bullets, small and pinpoint.
His arms are like guns, solid and always ready.
His anger is like thunder, roaring with passion.
His feet are like bombs, banging when he marches.
His fear is like a bull, when he sees red.
He has a heart like a martyr, everlasting in people's hearts.
His nerves are of steel, never bending in the heat.
His hair is short, maybe like his life.
Bang!

Daniel Cutting (13)
Edmonton County Lower School

THE HUNTRESS

She stalks prey eagerly,
Waiting to pounce.
Licking her lips in pleasure,
As the rabbits scuttle silently.

One wanders from the crowd,
She creeps through the smoky grass,
She pounces, she devours . . .
Nothing but shredded skin and fur.

She slinks away satisfied,
All is well, but not for long,
She hears the pounding of boots,
She is startled, she runs.

It is useless,
She hears a shot, she feels it.
She stumbles to the ground,
She gasps for air.

There is no point,
She is down, she is bloody,
Nothing but death.

No home for her cubs,
No mother to teach,
They are too young to fend,
They too shall perish like she.

Hooves tramp near her head,
They laugh, they kick her,
And they are gone.
The empty body is surrounded,
They scratch and tear at it.
She is devoured,
Fox to rabbit, dog to fox . . .

Rebecca Oyetey (12)
Edmonton County Lower School

BEST FRIENDS

Maybe you have one of these,
Maybe you have more,
To these you share your secrets with,
Cry your heart out to them behind a closed door.
You have good laughs with these,
They cheer you up when you're sad and blue.
You scream, giggle and shout with these.
They offer you their shoulder to cry onto.
You sigh together over lost loves,
Giggle together over crushes,
Cry together over sad films,
Argue together over blushers.
You can send them away with a cross word,
And bring them back with an apology.
They listen better than parents do,
And they nick the answers off you for biology.
Best friends are a good thing to have,
They can last a lifetime,
Or they can last five minutes.
If you give to them what you want back,
Their friendship, loyalty and trust won't lack.

Ruth Illsley (13)
Edmonton County Lower School

CRASH

I'm trapped in and I can't get out,
My voice doesn't seem to want to shout.
And there's many thoughts swimming round my head,
I can't hear my sister, I pray she's not dead.
There's a throb in my head as I try to turn round,
And I try to cry out but there isn't a sound,
Just a gurgling noise as I spit out the blood,
Then all the memories come back like a flood.
There was lots of drinking and the music was loud,
When we got to it, there was quite a crowd.
Whose house it was in, I hadn't a clue,
We didn't stay long, just an hour or two.
But on the way home, I didn't quite see,
The joyriders racing towards me.
Now I'm being pulled out from the front seat,
And my face is covered with a clean, white sheet.
Then my pain is gone and I feel so light,
When I gain back my vision everything's bright.
And I soon realise that I'm floating up high,
My heart breaks as my sister starts to cry.
An invisible tear trickles from my eye,
And to my heartbroken sister I say goodbye.

Stacey Hockley (13)
Edmonton County Lower School

I Know About Love, I'm In It!

Whenever someone talks to you and you're paying attention
To every minor detail, even if they ever mention
Politics, the weather, topics uninteresting
You stay with them when they go on about something depressing
If you still sit in awe of them with your mouth wide open
You think about your wedding day and yes, you might start hoping
That this person you're talking to is not attached at all
You've fallen in love madly and it's right in love you fall

If you think someone's gorgeous in a 'shot' with half their head
The picture's pretty ruined and you still think they're 'drop dead'
Their expression is cheesy and you still find yourself saying
'I pray to God one day on the same bed as you I'm laying!'
When you've not seen them in the flesh for ages, still you wonder
If when you marry, your hair would look better up or under
It's serious proof that if your body tingles when they call
You've fallen in love badly and it's right in love you fall

When all you talk about is the object of your desire
When you're off your head and thinking of them gets you higher
When they're talking rubbish, all you do is understand
You wouldn't drop your sweetheart for another girl or man
If you have pictures of them in your purse or in your wallet
And you know it's not 'obsession'
Though that's what the 'experts' call it
The feelings that you get for them can't be described at all
That's when you fall in love with them, that's right in love you fall.

Natalie Mott (13)
Edmonton County Lower School

DON'T DO IT!

I didn't know,
I didn't mean it,
I didn't know it would affect so many people.
I felt so bad afterwards.
I felt like screaming.
How could I do something so terrible,
And kill so many animals?
So many were killed,
One with its throat slit and one with glass in its paw.
Why, why did I do it?
I had no excuse.
It was me, I'm ashamed to say it.
Who threw it on the floor.
A glass bottle, a crisp packet,
And so much more.
Now I'm alone all in my room,
And I've got one message to all of you,
Don't do it!

Sinem Halil (12)
Edmonton County Lower School

THE SHIP OF DREAMS

The Ship of Dreams they called it,
It will never sink they said,
Now most of the people on that ship,
Are under the sea, dead.

Not enough lifeboats for everyone,
But they still left anyway,
Hit an iceberg in the ocean,
And watched all the lives float away.

Mothers and children in lifeboats first,
Split up from family and friends,
The question on everyone's lips,
'Will I ever see you again?'

The boat snapped in half,
Then bobbed up and down for a bit,
The other half of the boat sank,
Ending with the bit that was jagged and split.

The Ship of Dreams they called it,
It will never sink they said,
Now most of the people on the Titanic,
Are under the sea, dead.

Sophie Slater (14)
Edmonton County Lower School

MUSIC IS

Music comes in many guises
Classic, pop, reggae, rap
Man, woman, girl and boy
For endless plight, sorrow and joy
Around the world, throughout the times
You'll hear the familiar chimes.

Backing tracks, dance tracks, politics and prayer
Black, white, rich, poor - people everywhere
New, old, soft or bold
You may not be aware
Music is the food of love
A passion for us to share.

The power of music is undeniable
Creating moods of joy and fear
Adrenaline rush, rhythmic pulse
Providing tones of pleasure
Vibrations arranged - not by chance
A priceless wealth of treasure.

Imagine a world without music
Films without soundtracks
Emotions felt, expressions seen
Are day to day facts
Music is the food of love
Play on before it fades out.

Renan Hussein (14)
Edmonton County Lower School

ENDANGERED SPECIES

The golden eagle, the barn owl too
What have they ever done to you?
The tiger, the rhino and panda bear
Soon we won't see them anywhere.

The elephant, the tall giraffe
Majestic in their size,
But man gets a gun and just for fun
Shoots between the eyes.

The fish, the seals, the humpback whale
So agile in the sea
But man still gets the better of them
Why can't they let them be.

The red squirrel and the dormouse who
We must keep safe and sound
Big or small, we must treasure them all
They are precious to our world.

So I'm begging you as you go on your way
Please listen to what I have said
If we don't care and I'm not trying to scare
These creatures could soon all be dead.

David Weekes (14)
Edmonton County Lower School

I KILLED THE KING

I believe I'm the strongest hunter around.
I thrive to kill the king
That roams in these parts of its town.

My rifle is ready
And I seek the skin so deep.
My heart races as I think of the fun.

Through my binoculars
I see my money
Camouflaged by the golden sand.

I take a shot,
His body drops,
I put my truck into gear,
And speed toward the lying corpse.

I feel a rush,
As I reach for my knife
And stab just to make sure.
I put away my blood covered knife
And reached for one bigger.

I open its jaws,
Cut out all its teeth
And put them in my basket,
Blood fills its mouth,
I laugh with anticipation.

Slowly I cut off its skin,
Excitement climbs up my bones,
As the blood's pouring all over me.
I am covered with the lion's blood,
It makes me feel dangerous.
I just shove the skin at the back of my truck.

The sweetness of the lion skin trade.

Vanisha Mistry (12)
Edmonton County Lower School

MY BOYFRIEND

The day I saw him I wanted him to be mine,
I talked about him all the time.
The day my friends said please shut up,
I just carried on because I loved him too much.
That day he asked me to be his,
And I repaid him with a lovely kiss!
We hugged all day, we hugged all night,
Until that night he gave me a fright.
When he began to joke around,
And told me he was leaving town.
I thought I would die and started to cry,
And then I found out it was all a big lie.
But I don't know what I would have done,
Because he was my number one.
He started to wipe away my tears,
And began to whisper in my ears,
I love you so much, I really do care,
And I will look after you whenever you get scared.
This was my boyfriend, the one I loved,
He reminded me of a beautiful dove.

Nadine Hart (13)
Edmonton County Lower School

COMMON FEARS

I have grown up now.
My crib's too small for me.
It's time for my first bed.
I suppose I am looking forward to it,
But I am not sure, I am a bit worried.
I don't know what to think.
It will be here in a minute,
In the corner of my room.

It's here. I can't believe it.
There it is in the corner of my room.
The bed looks inviting.
Underneath doesn't,
It's dark and scary.
I'm sure I can see a pair of eyes,
Yes, there is, they are staring at me.
I don't know what to do,
        Where to go.

It's gone.
My eyes must be playing tricks on me,
A wave of relief washes over me,
But I still don't want to go to bed.

It's bedtime now, but I don't want to go upstairs,
But I have to.
I'm in my room now,
I can see those eyes again,
I'm scared.
I am sure it's a monster,
It's going to get me, I'm going to die!
Help!
The light's on.
It's over now,
I'm still scared but I will get over it.

Megan Hallsworth (12)
Edmonton County Lower School

THICK BLACK CLOUDS

Drugs are like a dream, strong, nothing
can get in your way.
Never-ending dream.
Needles are a-stabbing to the heart.
Drugs are like a lover, always there by your side.
Drugs are like poison, waiting to kill.
Drugs are an addiction, once you start you can't stop.
One day happy, as bright as the sun.
The next day glum like thick black clouds.
Drugs are like a bunch of sweets,
There's always one more to take.
Drugs are like a roller-coaster going up and down.
Drugs are a key to another life.
Drugs are murderers.
Drugs are *Death.*

Laura Mercer (13)
Edmonton County Lower School

THE WORLD

You can't ever put the world
Under the wing of the dove.
Nor can you silence the
Toys of corrupt children.
It just won't happen.

Poverty is the fool's gold of the world
There's plenty of it.
Too many wars are fought
Because of the greed of the dictators
This just happens.

Can't we just live in
Peace with the world?
Do we have to suffer
On behalf of others?
Why does this have to happen?

We can stop it
In its tracks.
All we have to do
Is avoid the facts
Of the world!

David Priestley (13)
Edmonton County Lower School

A LIFE ENDING!

Drugs are like a dream that never ends,
Drugs are like poison waiting to kill,
Needles are like a knife, stabbing to the heart,
Drugs are like a lover, there wherever you go,
Drugs are like chocolate, you can easily get addicted,
Drugs are like a lover that won't let go,
You're so unpredictable, one day you're fine,
Next you're ripping yourself apart,
Drugs will blow your mind away,
Drugs are like a key to a new life,
Drugs are like a bunch of sweets,
Always one more to try,
Drugs are like a thief, they steal your life away.

Rebecca Emery (14)
Edmonton County Lower School

THE CUTTING DOWN OF TREES

What is the point of another table or chair,
Wood, wood, it's everywhere,
But not for very long,
The few animals that are left,
 The sadness of their song.
Wood, wood, it's everywhere,
But not for long,
The beautiful trees are slowly going,
Going,
Going,
Gone.

Hayley Stevens (12)
Edmonton County Lower School

THE TELEPHONE

The telephone is never alone,
An object that has much to say.
Its loud cries to get your attention,
Are heard in all the rooms and in the lounge way.

The telephone is like a spy,
That listens to you talk and cry.
It listens to you everyday,
Listening to every word you say.

The telephone is a strange creature,
It's like trying to get through to an angry teacher.
You are always put on hold,
And your say is never told.

Is it really listening?

The telephone is a friend as well,
It helps you talk to others.
It helps you and everyone,
Especially gossiping mothers.

Yiannis Panayi (14)
Edmonton County Lower School

THE ELEPHANT

Here is where she used to stand,
Eat, drink and graze,
Feeling and looking after her young,
All throughout the day.

She did no wrong,
Nothing but good,
She and her mate, for here they stood,
Before that bloody day.

She didn't take her eyes off her young,
For they were her pride and joy,
She loved them so,
And showed it, in so many ways.

Never lonely was she,
With her mate and her calves,
But gone is she, here no more,
For they came with their guns and knives,
And took her in their graspful hands.

Kai Shayler (12)
Edmonton County Lower School

THE WARDROBE

I sit there day and night
watching and hoping someone
will look at me.
The young girl opens me
she takes out her clothes.
I have kept her clothes warm
and clean.

I've lived here all my life.
A woman cleans me once a week.
I can't bear to see the girl with
nothing to wear.
The new outfits go straight to me.

I am their slave
acquiring and donating their clothes.
I would like to be treated as
a human being,
the same as that little girl.

Louisa Mali (13)
Edmonton County Lower School

THE SCARY FOREST

I sit and stare at the forest,
Too scared, too scared to go in.
But something in my mind told me what to do,
It said, 'Go in, go in, go in.'

I heard a scary owl,
Then I heard some people coming,
I hide behind some bushes,
And see some men walking by.
They were holding bows and arrows,
And dressed in funny clothes.

I got up and decided to go,
And I made sure I kept very low.
I turned around and saw the trees,
Much, much more than before.
I started to get worried,
I started to get scared,
I started to run, and run, and run.

I suddenly stopped and saw the men,
Coming, coming closer,
I screamed and ran,
And ran and ran,
And never, never stopped running.

Lydia Mousoullou (13)
Edmonton County Lower School

FEAR

I'm sometimes here
and sometimes not
for I can be everywhere
that you are not.
I could be in a dream
for I am fear
and you can never escape from me.

For I can be a demon
in your dream,
I can be an old relative
who died in your dream.

For I am fear
and fear I'll be,
I will always creep up on you
in your sleep
till you get rid of me.

I'm evil and evil I'll be
so I can scare you,
till you get rid of me.

Goodbye my friend
till we meet again,
you have got rid of me
so I must go
and steal some other dream.
Goodbye my friend,
from fear, fear, fear, xxx.

Samantha Wilson (13)
Edmonton County Lower School

THE NAIL VARNISH

The house is a mess
She looks around the house
Grinning
At her lovely vain life.

She loves her way of living
Glamour and colour
She loves a lot of fashion.

She loves going to parties
Until all hours of the night
As she catches the light
Men stop and stare at her.

Shelley Lodge (13)
Edmonton County Lower School

THE TELEPHONE

The telephone sits comfortably still like a stone,
It's waiting for someone to ring,
Buttons hard as pennies, waiting to be pressed
And the receiver hoping to be picked up.

Inside the phone is an electric mind
Keeping secrets of conversations.
Chitter, chatter, chitter, chatter.

Suddenly it begins to ring.
Excitement in the air, hello, . . . wrong number.

David McGhie (13)
Edmonton County Lower School

LIFE GOES ON . . .

There's a hole in my life,
   now that he's gone.
He was my best friend,
   my whole life long.
It now seems strange without him here,
   it's almost been one whole year.
With him, I shared my hopes, my dreams,
   life will be harder, or so it seems.
But really life does go on,
   so I'll have to cope with him now gone.

Sarah Small & Emily Yates (13)
Edmonton County Lower School

MY SO-CALLED LIFE

I receive homework every weekday,
It takes up my time in every way.
Do you know what this means to me?
I have no life, you have to agree!
Weekends are supposed to be my day of rest,
But no, I end up revising for a test.
I like going to school and hanging with my mates,
I'll appreciate it in the end, a little hard work is all it takes!

Melissa Bhikoo (13)
Edmonton County Lower School

A PART OF ME

To you I gave a part of me,
I thought you felt it too,
But now I know, deep in my heart,
It probably was not true.

For love is blind, but you could always see,
Yet when I hurt, you lost your sight,
And now you're lost to me.

For as you're gone, out of my life,
As if without a trace,
And now you've left, behind has stayed,
Where you once filled a space.

You never knew, and never will,
The tears I cried for you,
But now I hope, that soon one day,
The pain, you'll know, I knew.

Now gone from me, and not returned,
For all the tears I've cried,
And now I am alone, it feels,
A part of me has died.

Zoë Moss (17)
Hendon School

NIGHTMARE

When I melt into a slumber, before I fall asleep,
My head full of desires, lets my poor heart weep.
My heartache from a past life and my longing for the future,
All bind together, to become a torture.

I am in a nightmare now,
And begging to get out.
I never wanted all this pain,
That has now come about.

I sweat and start to hit my bed,
To get these thoughts out of my head.
And finally they're out and gone,
I'm all safe now, but something's wrong.

The thoughts are still inside my head,
All those thoughts I truly dread.
But now I know just what I've done,
I've finally faced my fears head on.

I finally decide to rest my head,
Upon the pillows on my bed.
My body suddenly goes tense with fear,
What if my dream chooses to reappear.

But why would it choose to reappear,
'Cause now I know I have no fear.

Klara Brennan-Bernatt (13)
Highbury Fields School

LOVE LOSS
(Dedicated to the one I love Wayne Bannerman - WIISIC97)

I hated you at first,
But gradually I began to fall in love.
I had a tingle in my stomach
Each time I saw you.

This made me realise how I really did love.

Your big blue eyes threw me across the room,
Trapped.

This made me realise how I really did love.

My heart began pounding,
Like Linford Christie,
Running across the track.

This made me realise how I really did love.

My love for you filled my heart,
In each and every way,
And each time I saw you was like a sunset,
Going up instead of going down.

This made me realise how I really did love.

Everything suddenly changed,
When Daddy came back.
It had to end for no reason, or why.

This made me realise how I really did love.

And still we're together after a long few months.
And my heart grows bigger.
Filled with love and no hate.

This made me realise how I really did love.

All I know is this is a great deal of loss.

Catherine Louise Vitry (13)
Highbury Fields School

MAKING THE TEAM

Everyone pointing and shouting at me,
I had done it, only I could see,
All I did was kick a ball,
Everyone shouted 'It's two all!'
I wasn't part of the game,
But everyone seemed to know my name.
The pitch looked really muddy and quite cold,
One by one they began to call,
'Quick Kelly go and get the ball,'
Excited and happy they all seemed to be,
All because of someone like me.
Then I scored one more time,
This one from the halfway line,
We had won the game I knew for sure,
But I really couldn't score no more,
I was hot and red,
I really, really did need my bed.
Then when I woke it was only a dream,
If only it was real, I would have made that team!

Kelly Mills (14)
Highbury Fields School

CHRISTMAS TIME

Christmas time is exciting with the presents under the tree,
All the decorations glowing all of them Christmasy.
The carol singers at the door singing joyful songs,
They look warm and cosy but I know they're freezing cold.
I hang my stocking on the fire,
It's empty as can be.
But I know that in the morning it would be filled up to the brim.
I can't wait till Christmas comes,
All those presents for me.
What will I get? What will they be?
Who's to know but the people who got them for me?
I've got butterflies in my tummy and I'm running up and down,
I try to lose my energy,
But I just keep falling down.

April Hodges (13)
Highbury Fields School

STANDING IN THE SPOTLIGHT

Walking up to the block,
the feeling of being watched,
twenty-eight eyes staring,
knowing you're going red.
Standing in the spotlight, shaking,
reading out the poem,
the relief of finishing,
out of the spotlight.

Joanna McGavin (14)
Highbury Fields School

PLAYGROUND TORMENTS

The big sixth years come,
They come with their mates,
Me a small first year has no one,
I'm a state!

I roam around the playground as if I'm looking for a soul,
Hoping the big ones don't see me,
In case they make me fall.

I see them in the corner,
Stealing other children's money,
They don't seem to care and are too big to fear.

But they were one themselves,
Not so long ago.
They simply must have forgotten,
How else won't they know?

When I become a sixth year,
I will try to take the time,
To spare the little feelings,
Of the small first year,
Who finds life has no meaning.

Adeola Aderibigbe (13)
Highbury Fields School

I'M SO AFRAID

Sitting, waiting
second by second.
Eyes staring with disappointment and disapproval.
Me dying of shame and disappointment.

I should not have done it!

Noises of feet,
the sound of the army?
Hoping and waiting for someone to find me.
Voices of hatred filling the room,
when was somebody coming to get me?

Chewing gum everywhere,
God, what a state!
Hunger filling my stomach with ache.
Under this table I sat still in shock,
my head telling me danger
but was this true?

Oh God, what shall I do?

Soumaya Amrani (14)
Highbury Fields School

PURE POETRY

Poems can come in many different ways
They can lock you in a time capsule
They can leave you in a daze.

You will be left inside another world
Until your poem has ended
And when it does
You will feel as if your vocab's been extended.

You will find that each and every poem
Is different in a way
With some of them you feel at home
With others far away.

The flowing, drifting dialect
Can catch you unaware
And drag you down to no man's-land
Until the end of your poem is there.

Niamh Brennan-Bernatt (12)
Highbury Fields School

FEAR

I crawl into bed, off goes the light
I can tell straight away they'll be here tonight
The shadows returned, the noises begin
The ghosts are on the patio, drinking their gin
The clock struck twelve, the storm began
Thunder rolled, the figures have come
Tapping on the window, what could it be?
Is it the trees? I just can't see
Someone's coming up, the stairs start to creak
Or are they downstairs, I hear the taps leak
I crawl into bed, off goes the light
I can tell straight away I'll have nightmares tonight.

Samantha Allen (13)
Highbury Fields School

LOVE OF MY LIFE

Ever since that night
I liked you from the start
I wanted to be with you
And for us to never part

As I looked into your eyes
I knew you were meant for me
And our love to last forever
That's how I want it to be

I never realised until now
How much I care or
How much I want to share

To me you're really special
So gentle and so kind
I want us to be together
Your love I want to find

So what does it mean?
Can you really see?
Keep a space in your heart
For the one and only me.

Donna Padfield (14)
Highbury Fields School

THE POEM OF LIFE

That's what everyone says,
Life's nothing,
It brings you nothing,
It's born with nothing,
It never gives you any hope,
It lets you die with sadness.
In your inner self,
Life leaves the world in darkness.

But others say,
Life brings you heaps,
Life is born with a lot of use,
But can only watch you,
Suffer, but not reach out for you.

All life is waiting for,
Is more eagerness.
Life expects you to do it,
That's what life is for.
For you to make the most of it,
As I've said, it's the poem of life that makes people think.

That's when life begins.

Ayrun Nessa Begum (13)
Highbury Fields School

PARTY AWAY!

I went to a party, and I was going mad,
Until it all went bad,
I started dancing,
Until my feet felt like I was sinking in sand,
Before I knew it I was up again dancing with a lad,
I sat down again and I just felt sad,
So I just had to go mad!
So here I am not partying and just,
Sitting down writing this poem,
Asking Dad if it's good or bad?

Funda Civelek (14)
Highbury Fields School

INVISIBLE

Sitting there,
Sits an outcast,
Ignored all day,
Ignored all life,
Sitting there.

So cold,
So lonely,
Sits a talented person,
Wasting his talent away.

Tooting away,
On his lonely flute,
The chords flying past people's ears,
For they do not want to hear,
A wasted talent,
As invisible as the tramp.

Fred Sorrell (13)
Highgate School

COLOURS OF KALEIDOSCOPE

A myriad of colours,
Bursting vibrantly with life,
Is everywhere around us,
In peace and war and strife.

The sanguinary red,
In wartimes where
Much innocent blood is shed,
But then in summer
The rose does bloom and peace spreads a rumour.

Then, the ghastly hue of black,
Of treachery and corruption,
Has foolishly brought wartimes back.
But it's also the colour of grief and mourning,
Laments of a bygone age, which also heralds a dawning.

Then, the azure haze of blue,
Right down, to the depths of the seas.
It fills our life with many virtues,
But its sibilant oratory,
Soars up to the skies, and is revealed in a splendour of glory.

Then, the lush serenity of green,
Of pastures new, of peace.
Though grass, fills the land with an unearthly sheen.
But lurking under tranquillity,
Is a raging feral savagery, and immense antiquity.

The innocence of white,
Is the mantle of purity,
Where saintliness abides,
Pure, without blemishes,
Perfection itself, and the hope each one of us cherishes.

Ken Wee (13)
Highgate School

THE FIRST WORLD WAR

And now we wait in bunkers,
Ready to attack,
For the captain to give the signal,
Which was a pat on the back;
The captain gave the signal,
We went over the top,
We crawled as fast as we could,
So we didn't get shot.

And now we enter no man's-land,
Which we are not allowed in,
But we will do it anyway,
Because we want to win;
The German sniper spotted us,
With his single eye,
I hope he doesn't aim for me,
Because I will surely die.

And now retreat after setting the mines,
Which our captain told us to do,
One of our men said 'Well done' to me,
And I said 'You too';
We had won that battle victoriously,
Which was good for us,
Now we will go to another battle,
They will take us there by bus.

Sam Schneider (13)
Highgate School

WAR

War . . .
Politics, religion, territory, power, violence, pain, blood, tears.
What does it solve?
Who does it involve?
How long does it last?
When will it be in the past?
How many people does it hurt?
How many people does it satisfy?
War takes away the innocent
And those it leaves behind
Are left with nightmares and scars.
Peace is the precious jewel we're after,
We want to run free and hear our children's laughter.

Nawel Belmouloud (16)
Hornsey School For Girls

WAR AND PEACE

No peace through the night,
will you end the fight?
Where is the white dove
that brings peace and love?
Why must there be war?
Can't you see we are poor?
Your bombs took our shops,
please will you alter your filthy tone
and just leave us alone.
The other countries really tried
but the awful fact they cannot hide
is that this war will never end
so will you stop and be my friend?

Monica Singha (13)
Hornsey School For Girls

WAR

Why?
Everybody asks themselves
But only on Remembrance Day.
What is it we are remembering, who?
Was it a necessary evil?
Maybe it could have been prevented
'Oh what a lovely *war*', was a play I saw
I think
I know
It was lovely wasn't it?
Suffering, sad, sickening.

Why? Death, doom, darkness.
How - blood
How - wounds
How - corpses
'Lovely'
'Oh what a lovely war'
Cold, scared, alone,
Lovely, lovely, lovely, lovely,
Isn't it
Is it not
Not is it
It is.

Veronica Hoggar (17)
Hornsey School For Girls

MIST OF OUR DESIRES

As it filters into my soul,
Uncontrolled,
Unnoticed
Apart from the waves
Crashing upon my shores.
Eroding,
Destroying
As the surface slyly slides away,
Layer
By layer
I feel you slipping through my fingers.
Slowly,
Surely
As the burning in my stomach,
The flitter-flutter in my chest
As I hold you and kiss you,
Over and over,
Longer and harder.
Till all that remains
Is the mist of our desires.

Sara Stafford-Williams (17)
Hornsey School For Girls

I CAN SEE

Through the wind I can see your strength,
Through the rain I can see your tears,
Through the storm I can see your gentleness,
Through your emotions I can hear my music.

Lydia El-Aabdi (11)
Hornsey School For Girls

YOU

I wasn't looking for love.
You breezed in
From round the corner,
In your blue sports car.
Entering my life in a bubble of CK scent.

Cute like a five year old,
Yet hypnotising as was Juliet to Romeo.
Cheeky yet intelligent,
For a PC whiz kid.
Your footy club took you to the
Spanish plains, away from me.

Your charm weaved a web,
Alluring me closer to the forbidden fruit.
Your love made a deep impact
Igniting that untouched flame in my heart.

Vidya Mohit (18)
Hornsey School For Girls

AUTUMN

As the robin starts to sing its early morning song
I gaze down at the dew nestling on nature's carpet,
glistening like thousands of reflective crystals,
                        precious and worthy of a king.
Scarlet roses, with their velvety frail petals, devoured by
                        Jack Frost in the depths of the night.
The wind whistles past my ears shaking burnt orange and
                        cranberry-red leaves to their fate.
Golden pears dangling from trees are the pot of gold awaiting
                        you at the end of the rainbow.

Emily Dalton (12)
Hornsey School For Girls

TEACHER TALK

Sit down, shut up
Get on with your work,
I don't care at all
Even if she called you a jerk.

Now turn the page
Read down the line,
And don't bend the book back
You'll crack its spine.

I heard that boy!
Think you're so great,
You've got a detention
And don't dare be late.

Look at that skirt
It's far too short,
If you don't pull it down
I'll see you in court.

It wasn't like this in my day
All this hip hop chatter,
Pull yourselves together
Good heavens what's the matter.

I don't know why they shout
And shout and shout and shout,
I'd really give a lot to know
What it's all about.

Mikhaila Fam (11)
Hornsey School For Girls

I WONDER WHY?

I wonder why
I wonder why
people make me cry
it's 'cause of my colour

All people should think about is kindness
kindness to fill their world
kindness to fill their dreams

It doesn't matter if people are black or white
just respect their colour 'cause that is right
it doesn't matter if people are black or white
just be friends and don't start a fight

I wonder why
I wonder why
people make me cry
it's 'cause of my colour

All I wanted to say is that racism is not the right word
it doesn't matter if you're black or white
just be friends and hold tight

Racism spoils everything
racism spoils everything we want
why do we have to be so bad
and why do we have to be so sad

Racism spoils our future
racism spoils our world
racism ruins our lives
so
just drop the knife and live your life.

Derya Yilmaz (13)
Hornsey School For Girls

THE PERFECT SCHOOL

One day I went to school,
Feeling really, really cool,
When suddenly I looked through the school gate,
This isn't . . . wait . . .
The school was transformed,
Sparkly and bright,
My school looked so pretty, so perfect, so right!
I spoke to all my teachers,
They knew no more than I did
It must be a miracle I later on decided.

Layla Richardson (11)
Hornsey School For Girls

UNDONE

I sit here, trying to write this poem,
My mind is blank,
I stare at the ground.
This is where we had walked once,
Together,
But now, it is the same ground,
We tread on it,
Separately.
I think on . . .

Rehana Khatun (18)
Hornsey School For Girls

THE SUNSET

The sunset begins to set
The sea begins to cool
People begin to swim while
The waves begin to fall

The sea begins to set while
The sky begins to change
to yellow, to orange and to blue
People begin to put on their clothes

The sky is getting darker
From blue to black
And now the night begins.

Rajmin Ali (13)
Hornsey School For Girls

LIFE

Life is hard like a hot big pan.
Oh I wish somebody could give me a hand,
on this very hard land.

I want money
we all say but the money never
but the money never comes this way
oh why we all say
in a very angry way.

Fiona Boateng (11)
Hornsey School For Girls

THE MOON

A milk-white porthole,
The 'lunar phenomenon' alias the moon.
It's the same every night;
The sun sets and the moon takes over for the night shift.
An ivory beacon gleaming as if it will never stop,
A welcome relief from the eerie darkness.

Everywhere is calm and serene,
Nothing moves and tranquillity takes control.
The world sleeps.

Until . . .

. . . Dawn catches up with night,
And the last gentle moonbeams shimmer and fade,
Into tomorrow.

The first refreshing rays of morning sunlight peep through my
                                        curtains and dazzle me.
The sun sets in,
And the world yawns and awakens.

Lottie J Hamer (12)
Hornsey School For Girls

I LIKE THE FILM TITANIC

I like the film Titanic
The film is so fantastic
I've seen the film 3 times
I still see it in my mind
Nothing on earth can come between them
Apart from the iceberg that sank them.

Hoi-Ling Li (12)
Hornsey School For Girls

MY FIRST DAY

I hold on tightly to my mum
We walk into the nursery
I feel safe and secure
But everything is so big, so strange
Then Mum has to go home
I beg her not to
But she does
I burst into tears
The other children are fine, but I am not
They have their own friends
I am all alone
By myself
Lonely
Then a girl calls me over
We talk, we play
Now I have a friend
I am no longer lonely
Mum comes back
I tell her about my new friend
I can't wait until tomorrow.

Sophia Awan (12)
Hornsey School For Girls

WHY ARE PEOPLE?

Why are people cruel and unkind?
Why don't people use their mind?
Do they find pleasure in being unfair
Or is it that they just don't care?

Why don't people think twice
Before taking away a person's life?
Don't they think about consequences
Because life has great expenses?

Are people mean for fun
Or to them is life a constant drum?
Is it like a game
Or do they just want fame?

Either way it should stop!
Because life is precious it can't just go *pop!*

Shamim Mussa (12)
Hornsey School For Girls

MY FRIENDS!

My friends are really mad,
Some of them are really bad
They never behave
They love to rave
And then they say I'm mad.

They really hate boys
And make loads of noise
Oh my gosh
They'll drive you mad.

They're really rude
And eat with their fingers
They keep telling me
They want to be singers.

I can't imagine what they would do
If they were famous, it can't be true.
They think they're grand,
I don't understand.

Am I one of them?

Emma Gullick (12)
Hornsey School For Girls

THE HONEYSUCKLE

When the honeysuckle bloomed,
my dad would pick me up
whenever I fell over.
I would spend all day
having fun, running about.
But now the honeysuckle is losing its flowers to the frost.
And if I fall over I wipe my tears away
and pull myself up.

When the honeysuckle bloomed,
a friend was a friend,
and it was the end of the world
if my cup-cake fell on the floor.
But now the honeysuckle fights to survive throughout the
long, cold winter.
A cup-cake is the least of my worries,
and without a friend
your life is left shivering in a cold corner.

When the honeysuckle bloomed,
pain and tears were over in a second.
A second was a lifetime
and a pot of gold was under every rainbow.
But now the honeysuckle fights for a glimpse of sunlight
As the sun sleeps through the winter.
But now life is one big pain
which strides on forever
and I'd be lucky for a piece of coal.
But as I think about it
life isn't as hard as it could be
and soon it'll be summer again
and the honeysuckle will bloom and smell better than ever.

Rosie Housman (12)
Hornsey School For Girls

THE BEACH

I watch the sea
A dark blue sea
I wonder if it will come to me
A splinter of light
Shining so bright
I'm sad it will be gone by night
I look out into the distance
I see the sun set
I touch the sand so cold and wet,
Now everybody has gone home
And I'm all alone
It's such a peaceful place
I say with a smile on my face
It's so quiet I think
I can't hear a sound
Except those big waves crashing around
I sit and stare and a few moments pass
It seems like a lifetime when at last
Natalie, Natalie, someone's calling my name
And I know it's time to go
Still it's been a lovely day
I hope I can come again.

Natalie Andrew (13)
Hornsey School For Girls

MY KITTEN

My kitten was really bad,
but he likes my dad.

He sleeps on my bed,
his favourite colour is red.

He likes mice,
but sometimes woodlice.

He scares off my dog,
and likes the weather fog.

He plays outside a lot,
with my next-door neighbour plot.

He hates cars,
his favourite chocolate Mars.

He sometimes plays with me,
and hates my uncle Lee.

He likes pulling my hair,
his favourite animal is a bear.

And this was my kitten,
who lived in Britain.

Dipa Uddin (12
Hornsey School For Girls

OUR ROSES

We had such a lovely garden
full of sunny daffodils and red roses.

I can still feel the warm air
wrapping itself around us,
pushing us together
so close that I could feel your heartbeat
racing against time,
hoping that night
would last for eternity.

It feels as if
I've been watching our love
grow and blossom
through the window.

I've seen it being nourished
by passion and affection,
fed by devotion and tenderness.

But now
as I look out at the garden,
it looks so dead and lifeless.
The roses are just sanding there
all shrivelled up
like brown paper bags
that have been squished together.

As the years have gone by
our roses have been neglected.
They look so fragile and lonely,
hungry for vitality and attention.

Tamary Penlerick (17)
Hornsey School For Girls

LITTLE DID I KNOW I WAS IN FOR A SCARE!

Thinking of home, thinking of there,
While we were up in the air,
Thinking of Bro, Dad and Mom,
And what to buy for everyone,
Little did I know I was in for a scare,
While we were up in the air.

All of a sudden I heard the creek and crackle
Of the intercom and children screaming,
We're gonna crash, we're gonna crash,
Help us someone,
The teacher tries to calm us down,
While the plane speedily plunges down.

Putting on our life jackets and heading for the exit,
In the pit of my stomach I was gonna be sick,
We made it out and swam in the ice-cold sea,
It was the middle of the night and I could not see,
I swam and swam with all my might till I saw an island lit
                                        by moonlight,
I reached the shore and there I stayed,
Wondering if I'll live to see another day.

Teisha Bradshaw (12)
Hornsey School For Girls

AUTUMN IS HERE

As I was walking down the road today,
I noticed Autumn was on her way,
The wind was blowing gently,
The leaves were turning yellowy,
People were wrapping up,
In jumpers and in coats.

As I was coming home from school,
I noticed conkers on the ground,
I noticed hardly any sound,
No more blue skies till next year,
Witches' hats in shop windows,
As I walked up my road,
I noticed houses grey and cold.

As I got ready to go to bed,
I looked out of my window to see red,
Yellow, green in the sky,
Guy Fawkes is here.
Then all of a sudden rain starts to fall,
Street lights come on,
Clocks will soon be going back,
Now we wait until next year.

Lauren Beary (12)
St James' Catholic High School, Colindale

THE GRAND ARRIVAL

As I was walking down the road today
I noticed autumn on her way,
She was sparkling like fireworks on Guy Fawkes night
She was colourful like a tree with red, yellow and brown leaves
The sun was lowering in the sky
There was a newsagents with a witch's hat in the window as
I passed by.

The wonderful colours she was
Reminded me of dressing up on Hallowe'en
The smell of exhaust fumes in the air as the sun dies down
For we were in the middle of autumn when the clocks go back
People were trying to run away from her
People like to be warm.

Nightime had arrived
And autumn was ready to leave
But she had left something pretty
Something pretty like a queen's diamonds on her neck
Autumn had forgotten the frost
Over the horizon I could see someone bolder
It was male
It was winter.

Celia-Jane Ukwenya (12)
St James' Catholic High School, Colindale

130

AUTUMN IN THE CITY

September's here and autumn's by its side
This time of year the sun begins to hide
The colours come out green, yellow and brown
There is so much rain the flowers start to drown
All the leaves fall off the trees
And if you look around you'll see no wasps or bees.
On October 31st it's the day of Hallowe'en
This year I think I'll dress up as the killer from Scream.

Five days later it's Bonfire Night
All those fireworks will give your pets a fright
As you look up in the sky and see the fireworks flying high
Don't forget to give some money to the guy
When November comes autumn's nearly over
Oh what a pity it's the end of the poem Autumn In The City.

Jason Cianfrone (12)
St James' Catholic High School, Colindale

AUTUMN TURNING TO WINTER

Autumn in the city
It is really busy
The leaves are going gold
I am turning cold
I am playing in the snow
My brother doesn't want to know
My brother watches out the window to see if
anyone is coming for Hallowe'en.
We both look out so we both look at the fireworks
all night long.

Paul Doyle (12)
St James' Catholic High School, Colindale

CITY SEASONS

September rain, December snow where the sun went I don't know!
Summer sun it was such fun, the winds start to come, why oh why
did the summer heat fade,
People still let the summer music play even though autumn's here
and summer's faded away.
City street lights let the frost be seen,
Frost on windows starts to gleam.
The sound of darkness to be heard, no more singing from the birds.
It's Hallowe'en night in the city there are eggs on windows oh what a
pity.
People come from near and far just to get a chocolate bar.
Hallowe'en's over, oh what a shame the eggs on the windows, will I get
the blame.
Next to come is Bonfire Night, which gives all pets quite a fright.
The fireworks go up *bang!* Next it's Christmas and carols are sung.
I can't wait for the sun to come back out, I'm going on holiday without
a doubt.

Kieran Sexton (12)
St James' Catholic High School, Colindale

AUTUMN IN THE CITY

The days are getting shorter.
The nights are getting long.
Soon it will be farewell to
Summer's warm, sweet song.

The starlings flock together.
The leaves begin to fall.
The mellow autumn colours
Herald winter's icy pall.

In the park the grass is damp now,
The flowers are no more.
The squirrels rush in panic
To make their winter store.

The wet streets and pavements
Glisten with mist and frost.
The chill winds fade the memory
Of summer's glories lost.

Lisa Swann (12)
St James' Catholic High School, Colindale

KIDS IN THE AUTUMN

Autumn is nice and cold in the city of London,
With leaves and conkers falling off the trees,
With the kids picking up conkers to collect some,
Now with children going round trick or treating,
Some like witches, some like monsters but all the food,
All they collect will be nice and sweet and ready for the children to start
eating.

Then comes Guy Fawkes' Night, playing with fireworks,
Some kids earn the money for fireworks by penny for the guy,
But just remember, remember the fifth of November,
With gunpowder, treason and plot.
We see no reason why gunpowder treason should ever be forgot,
And all the things inside autumn should never be forgot.

And another thing, never play with fireworks,
Although it might be fun to stick them in your mates' pockets, it's not,
And then after all of autumn we will go back to the lovely clear sky
that summer will bring us.

Daniel Hernon (12)
St James' Catholic High School, Colindale

AUTUMN (IN THE CITY)

As I was walking to school one day,
I noticed autumn was on its way,
I saw an apple ripe to the core,
and then I saw a conker rolling on the floor,
All of the leaves are falling down from the trees,
blowing around in the autumn soft breeze.

In English class Mr Darcy says,
'Look at the trees, the leaves, look at them sway,'
In PE we're playing rugby,
I feel the cold gaining on me,
After school on my way back,
I look at the sky so very black.

Doing my homework, in the back room,
I feel a shiver down my spine,
I looked at my watch, it was nine,
I looked out of the window, did you know,
the chill down my spine was the white snow
I heard a bang and then another,
but it was just kids playing with some bangers.

Lee Kilcoyne (12)
St James' Catholic High School, Colindale

DESERT POEM

All I saw were trees
and big bumble bees,
I have no food
so what shall I do?

My head felt sore
I could do no more,
I later bled,
I felt as if I was going to be dead.

I dearly wished I was home,
so that I wouldn't be alone,
what I saw in sight
brought me such delight.

I saw a helicopter,
it was coming down,
I'm glad I didn't stay
and that I flew away.

Messiac Chaminda James (11)
St James' Catholic High School, Colindale

TO AUTUMN

It's dawn, I get up.
I can see autumn is here.
The leaves are falling on to people's cars.
The days are getting shorter
And the girls and boys are out playing
throwing leaves at each other.

You can see the horizon line
between the sunlit buildings and the glowing sky.
It's a typical cold autumn night
Just right for fireworks.
Me and my dad
just got back with some fireworks
so we're going to set the Catherine wheel alight
Whooh! It's wicked
It reminds me of the sun.

Myles McEneny (12)
St James' Catholic High School, Colindale

THE POEM

As I walk I watch the trees,
Swaying above the fallen leaves.
I see that autumn is on the way,
Because the sky is very grey
The city it is far too loud,
As for the city, well I'm not proud.

The trees have gone from green to brown,
As all the leaves die and fall down.
I walk over all the leaves,
They crack under my feet.

As I walk home from school,
I think of all the beer and joy
For Hallowe'en has not yet come,
But I know now that autumn is truly gone.

Chris Mannion (12)
St James' Catholic High School, Colindale

TO AUTUMN (IN THE CITY)

As I was walking down the road today,
I noticed autumn was on its way.
The leaves were rustling loud and clear,
It was a lovely sound that I could hear.
The cool autumn wind was blowing on my face,
It felt so different and out of place.
Summer was going now I didn't want it to end,
Hallowe'en was coming just around the bend.
I couldn't wait to get money and sweets,
And all other kinds of different treats.

November the fifth, Bonfire Night,
Don't get hit by a sparkler's light.
Be safe, don't be silly,
Don't aim fireworks at girls called Lilly.
All colours of the rainbow up in the sky,
When all the fireworks shoot up high
We have to put back all our clocks,
And wear heavy tights and socks.
Oh yes, I do like autumn coming,
Oh, I'm daydreaming, I'd better start running!

Siobhan Munroe (12)
St James' Catholic High School, Colindale

AUTUMN (IN THE CITY)

As I was walking down the road today
I noticed autumn was on its way
The trees were green and our school was clean
The leaves were swaying in the early autumn breeze
The buildings looked OK even though summer had gone away.

The hustle and bustle of the city streets,
The leaves are falling above my head,
And also scrunching under my feet.

And now autumn is nearly up,
The trees are bare,
But not in the square,
All the kids are screaming,
And the rain is teaming.

Paul McFadden (13)
St James' Catholic High School, Colindale

GETTING THROUGH AUTUMN

In the morning it is sometimes bright but cold
A slight breeze sends a chill down your back
I step outside it's not so bad
I see the street lights still on and hardly a leaf on the road.

It is now midday and it's lashing down with rain
The wind is strong, yanking leaves off trees, trying to make them bare.
Everyone riots trying to get into the warm so as not to get caught by the
bitter chill.

I now walk home, it's getting dark
There's an occasional bang and scream of fireworks
Once I get home the doorbell keeps ringing
And every time you hear the words, *'Trick or treat!'*

Stephen Brady (12)
St James' Catholic High School, Colindale

AUTUMN TO WINTER

When I wake up it's really cold,
But come lunchtime it's really warm,
When I come home it's really, really cold and frosty,
Then the fireworks come, *bang!*
It's fireworks night,
But before that it's Hallowe'en
Ghosts and witches come out again.

The clocks go back an hour,
Oh good an hour more to sleep in,
The leaves turn red and brown,
But the trees stay the same as always.

The houses are dark as I walk down the street,
Except for the street lights which light up the night,
The senses are sweet,
But sometimes are sour.

One day autumn's not there,
The trees go all bare,
Then I realise winter's here.

Ciara Clifford (12)
St James' Catholic High School, Colindale

TO AUTUMN (IN THE CITY)

It was a cold and bitter morning to start the day,
As I was walking I saw a tree,
The tree's once green leaves had disappeared
All dead and changing colours falling from the trees.

It was freezing now like an igloo.
The trees were burdened with all the deceased leaves.
It was so cold I felt ice-sharp spears thrust into my side
My face was frozen like diamonds on the Queen's neck
I wish I had a deckchair and the summer was back
I hear a distant cry, 'Trick or treat'
And loud bangs from memories of great battles past.

The Ice Queen is here in all her glory like a great warrior
Death and destruction lays in her path
Nothing stands in her way
The animals go into hiding, the insects die,
The pond freezes over
It was dusk and the night was near
All the children's' cheer has gone, they hide in their houses.
Soon winter will pass and summer will come again.

Timothy Meaney (12)
St James' Catholic High School, Colindale

To Autumn In The City!

As I was walking down the road today,
I noticed autumn was on its way.
As I looked up into the very high sky,
The dark clouds appeared before my eyes,
The cold breeze brushes upon my legs
As all the leaves crumble up and change into red,
Hallowe'en does draw near
Pumpkins, bats and spiders, people always love to cheer.

Be careful on bonfire night,
As you might get an awful fright,
All the beautiful colours in the sky,
The fireworks shoot up very high,
All the lights on in the streets
Everyone always meets
Longer nights and shorter days,
Everyone always wants to stay.

Snow, snow, falls to the ground,
As it does not make a sound.
Snowflakes flitter here or there,
Without any little care,
As people celebrate
Why is Christmas always late
At Christmas no one makes a sin
A new year will then begin.

Sharon Murphy (12)
St James' Catholic High School, Colindale

TO AUTUMN IN THE CITY

Summer is now starting to die,
While autumn is starting to rise,
Some of the leaves are still on the trees
But the floor is now golden-brown and white.
The apples around
That have fallen to the ground,
Have been harvested with the wheat and corn
But into the city,
It's not so pretty,
And now it's a very different story.

Into the hustle and bustle of the pattering feet,
The people stamp on the ground,
Not noticing the sound,
Of the leaves getting mushed into the floor.
The colours are not seen,
With all their gleam,
Because the fog covers them with its sooty blanket.

The sun is now not so bright,
But the wind still blows with all its might.
Busy people running round making more changes than the sound.
The days grow short and by the night
Fireworks glow and light.
Up in the sky they run about,
'Bang, clang, zang,' they shout.

Ewan Gillies (12)
St James' Catholic High School, Colindale

4To Autumn (In The City)

While walking down a road today,
I noticed autumn on its way,
Through busy roads and crowded streets,
Her dear friend, summer she did meet.
The fresh wind dancing round my legs
The trees painted with golds and reds.
As they shiver in the bracing breeze.

While walking later here and there,
I noticed autumn brush her hair,
And settle down to her long sleep,
Then next year out of bed she'll creep,
To start her cool season once more
And ripe the fruits all to the core
For winter has dawned and summer's set.

Or bats and witches, ghosts and ghouls
Children dressed up as scary fools
Welcoming Hallow's Eve
While others grieve,
At the loss of the sun
Yet more kids run to get their sweets
Farewell my friend autumn rest in peace.

Alexandra O'Neill (12)
St James' Catholic High School, Colindale

To Autumn In The City

As I walked down the road today, I noticed that autumn was on its way.
I felt a bit chilly, the leaves on the trees were changing colour and
falling down on to the ground
As midday was creeping on its way the sun was dying away behind the
grey clouds.
The clouds were lower than before.
I was missing summer but I could not wait until Christmas.

As I walked down the road, I noticed that autumn was on its way.
The mornings were getting darker and very cold
The fluffy clouds made us very sad and gloomy.
My hands didn't want to come out of my pockets, they just
wouldn't stay warm.
As I walked into school not many boys played football in the mornings.

As I walked out of class to get my lunch the leaves were changing
colour very fast.
The leaves were falling. People crunched leaves. They were laughing
and joking around chasing after the grey squirrel.
The lunch was very hot and warmed up my body.
As the school bell rang people were glad to be inside.

As I walked home the leaves were even crunchier and the ground was
brownish in colour.
It was quite dark. The little children dressed up for Hallowe'en, and
looked for money, sweets and other treats.

Lisa Maher (12)
St James' Catholic High School, Colindale

AUTUMN

Autumn is here summer is not,
The air is fresh and cool, not stuffy and hot.
Feel the breeze cold on your face,
And hear the rustling leaves as you walk on them.

Autumn colours everywhere,
Golden-brown, reds and orange here and there.
Witches' hats, bats and cats,
Decorated on every house.

Wrap up warm with scarves hats and gloves,
People with no coats shiver constantly,
Buying each other presents to put under the Christmas tree.
Christmas is here and it's getting close to New Year
So go inside and enjoy the party.

Emma Tuvera (12)
St James' Catholic High School, Colindale

AUTUMN ON IT'S WAY

As I was walking down the road today
I noticed autumn was on her way.

It was brown, yellow and green
With the light at night down at me.

As I carried on walking with the wind in my face
I looked up and saw a witches hat in the shop window.

I hear and see the sparkling fireworks
Like stars in the sky.

As the nights are longer and they days are shorter
I end up falling over by the open fire.

Mairèad Conway (13)
St James' Catholic High School, Colindale

AUTUMN VULNERABLE

It was wet and windy
and the showers were getting mischievous.
This early morning was looking hideous.
It was very grim,
everyone was looking dim.
The newsagents were jam-packed
with juveniles looking for fireworks
for that hair-raising festival coming up.
The leaves were scattered across the floor.
You could just about see the sycamore.
This maple tree was dying.
All the pensioners were sighing.
It started to drizzle.
You could hear the bacon in the cafe sizzle.
The morning was dawning,
all the cars were horning.
The sound was nearly deafening.

Dayo Olubodun (13)
St James' Catholic High School, Colindale

THE TRUTH ABOUT AUTUMN

As I was walking down the road I noticed autumn was on her way.
The brown and purple leaves were falling.
And you can hear the beautiful robin calling.

Hallowe'en is on its way,
All the children go out at night and play.
Wondering what they can seek
Some money, a sticker or better a sweet.

Now that autumn has gone
We hear Christmas carols so sing along.

Christopher Coffey (12)
St James' Catholic High School, Colindale

THREE SWEET SEASONS

Summer has gone and Autumn is here,
Autumn came slowly, slid its way quietly into the world.
Rotten fruits drop off trees and get squashed on the ground.
The breeze is soft but fairly cold.
Goodbye sweet summer, soon to be seen again.

Autumn! Such beauty! Golden, brown and red leaves
take place of the bittersweet fruits that once hung gently
in the warm breeze of summer.
The streets smell damp yet fresh.
As the cold air fills up your lungs
You can close your eyes and relax,
listening to the cold wind rushing through
the leaf-shredding trees.
Cats, hats and bats, witches' brooms and trick or treat,
Hallowe'en signals the end of autumn, soon to be seen again.

Winter! With its bitterness and frost! Cold, sharp breezes
and exaggerated bareness. Beautiful leaves are swept off
trees and in their place standing dying, bare branches.
Children happily singing Christmas carols, feeling the
familier tingling of excitement knowing that Christmas is drawing
near. Santa Claus is in their thoughts as they watch beautiful
snowflakes drifting down, taking their time - Why rush?
Winter is the true season of goodwill and happiness
And, we look forward to another year . . .

Sara Daoud (13)
St James' Catholic High School, Colindale

AUTUMN IS OUR MESSENGER

Her brown eyelids open
and her yellow bosom friends arise.
As she despatches, the leaves shiver
with fright, they change colour and sadly
fall down to the shriveled ground.
She blows her foul, soily breath through
a hollow, misshapen, naked tree to the plain
fields of St James.

      As she sits under an evergreen tree
she sees a young girl dressed in black.
'The hour has come, the hour of the witches
has begun,' Autumn thought. An old woman
came into presence and said,
'Come, come rejoice with me,
would you rather trick or be treated?'
'Autumn, who is she? Where did she
come from, and must she bring us the winter?'

      'I think they speak wrong, Autumn's
my friend and so mild, she's so fine and so in style.
She weeps with guilt for once was filth but through
regret she got upset and made a wheel, made out of steel.
What beauty, she is so tall and fine, with hair like
mine so live like five. Her nails so long they sing
a song and also played the game ping-pong.

      Autumn is so kind she warns us now,
Winter is here so pack your bags.
I know Autumn, she's my friend, she's so fine and
so in style.

Connie Abbe (12)
St James' Catholic High School, Colindale

To Autumn

When today I got out of bed
Outside summer was nearly dead
As I stepped outside,
A single leaf floated onto the drive
Summer is at its end
Autumn is round the bend.

A very small breeze
And the whistling wind winding in the trees
Their leaves are royal red, gold and brown
Because of their gentle frost, fitted jackets, I shan't get down
And I throw dead leaves into the air,
They come down and shower my hair.

Autumn is saying goodbye
Winter is saying 'Hi'
On this dark night great for *trick or treat*
You never know I might earn a sweet
The devil of doom
A witch on her broom
Bye bye autumn come back soon.

Siobhan Hackett (12)
St James' Catholic High School, Colindale

Desert Island!

I live on a desert island now,
even though there's nothing to do.
And around here you definitely
wouldn't see a kangaroo.

Straight away in the morning,
when I arise from my branched bed,
all the things I have ever done
are spinning around in my head.

I eat berries for my breakfast,
but most of the time it's brunch,
sometimes I eat breakfast and
it's nearly time for lunch.

In the evening I lie in my branched bed,
and look up at the stars,
then I fall asleep and
dream about cars.

Edel Gallagher (12)
St James' Catholic High School, Colindale

TO AUTUMN (IN THE CITY)

Autumn has arrived in the city,
It will be very busy
With everything going on.
These things like Hallowe'en, Guy Fawkes
Will be coming up soon,
Which will be really, really cool.

When Hallowe'en starts,
It will be cool,
With all the scares and things,
There will be lots of sweets involved
From people knocking at doors.
Saying trick or treat.

Guy Fawkes night will start after Hallowe'en
Which will be really, really busy
With people getting ready to buy
Noisy boxes of fireworks.

It is now Christmas time,
It is time for Autumn to go.

Jack Dennis Ryan (12)
St James' Catholic High School, Colindale

A DESERTED PLACE

The storm is like an angry lion waiting to pounce.
Suddenly it leaps upon us and the ship goes down.
Water surrounds me, when I get to the surface
I go down again.
Next thing, I wake up on a sandy seashore.

I feel so hungry and tired.
I don't know what to do with myself.
I go in search of food just to keep me going.
The sun is blinding and so hot.
I start to see things that aren't there.

My mind is full of fear and worry.
How am I going to get rescued?
Suddenly I remembered what I was taught
when I was younger.
'If you are in a spot of bother,
Help will come if you send a signal'.

As if by magic a bottle, some paper and a pen,
appeared by my worn out bare feet.
I started to write out my message.
When I had finished I put my message
in the bottle and sent it out to sea.

Within a few days I saw a ship coming towards me.
The boat had come to pick me up and take me home.
I was once again in my warm house
drinking tea and eating cake
in front of a warm roaring fire.

Tara Shanahan (11)
St James' Catholic High School, Colindale

LADY AUTUMN

She and her people started today,
At bringing in the chill and keeping the sun at bay.
She worked her magic onto the birds,
Swooping and looping, ducking and diving,
All going together like cattle in herds.

Away from the country and on through the town,
Where the leaves, scarlet and sorrel began to fall down,
On through the streets towards the town square,
Where the harvest was ripe and in abundance there.

She looks down to Earth, regal in her reign,
Starting off the drizzle, the blustery winds and the rain,
She smiles contentedly, she's completed her task,
'Roll on spring! Oh please,' we ask.

Michelle Coyle (12)
St James' Catholic High School, Colindale

AUTUMN COLOURS AND LIGHTS

My favourite time of year is autumn,
Hallowe'en with children running door to door,
Getting sweets and scary masks,
Throwing apples, rotten to the core,
Autumn is also a time of colours,
Brown on the trees, reds on the floor.

On Guy Fawkes night don't get a fright
Stand far back and watch the lights.
Sure they're loud and sometimes scary,
But with fireworks always be wary.

Daianne Cope (12)
St James' Catholic High School, Colindale

AUTUMN IN THE CITY

As I was walking down the road today
  I noticed autumn was on her way.
As the leaves fell down on me
  I heard a firework screech.
As I walked a shiver went down my spine
  I thought to myself where's that bed of mine.

As I walk into my house the warmth makes me smile.
  Sitting on my chair with my legs in a pile.
Just as I'm about to sleep
  I hear a knock on the door.
Slowly I rise and begin to creep.

I open the door slowly when to my surprise
  Three little children begin to cry
     Trick or treat
I thought to myself oh no not this again.
  Every year it's always the same
The kids play the same silly game.

I love this time of the year which some people fear,
  The cold snowy mornings and all those warnings,
But the thing I love most is all the Christmas post.

Stephanie Bohan (12)
St James' Catholic High School, Colindale

SEASONS OF THE CITY

The dying sun is in my view,
the leaves are starting to fall to the warm floor,
conkers rolling and mixing in with the leaves
which are crispy and brown,
A new wind is starting to blow now
into a thin breeze,
Travelling through the trees reaching speed,
Making the most of the last of summer,
children playing in the park,
soon they know it's going to get dark.

It's mid-autumn now and squirrels are chasing
each other while collecting acorns for winter,
while we are tucked in front of a burning fire
in our armchair.

It's starting to get cold now and as I breathe
warm air comes rushing out of my mouth,
snow is coming down from the heavens as cold
wet droplets of ice which melt in your mouth
when you stick your tongue out.
The snow is knee-deep now so I'm going inside.

James Sealey (13)
St James' Catholic High School, Colindale

ABANDONED

I woke up one day on a desert island,
so hot and tired was I.
I got up to where I was,
then I saw a whale swim by.
I looked out to sea and saw my ship sink,
as I took my golden tearful blink.
I plucked up the courage to go look around,
I could barely hear a single sound.
I began to wonder how I would survive,
and thought how to stay alive.
I then looked up to find a coconut tree,
then I realised I was as happy as can be.
I lived on that island until this very day,
I lived on coconuts until the month of May.
So what I'm trying to say is let your life shine,
then everything will be just fine.

Gina Grandfield (11)
St James' Catholic High School, Colindale

STRANDED

There I was stranded, scared and shivering
It was horrible, there was a terrible smell.
It was like being in the middle of hell.

The rain started falling on top of my head,
I wish I was home asleep in my bed,
I ran under a tree.
Oh, why did this happen to me.

I wish I was back at home
Instead I'm in the middle of a storm.

John Michael Mullen (11)
St James' Catholic High School, Colindale

DESERT ISLAND SUN

Desert island sun,
Having lots of fun!
Nothing to drink,
The sand and dust makes me blink!
Eating juicy fruit,
I hear the birds hoot!

Desert island coconuts
Sleeping in broken huts!
The storm was rough,
But I was tough!
I sheltered in a cave,
But with no adults around I don't have to behave!

Desert island slime,
And dirt and grime!
But the rest of the island's okay,
Especially in the day!
When it's nice and sunny,
And the animals are funny!

Desert island sounds,
And there's sand on the ground!
That's yellow and bright,
In the sunlight!
Desert island sun,
Having lots of fun!

Francesca Donno (11)
St James' Catholic High School, Colindale

I'M BORED

As I walked around the desert island,
My loneliness filled the air
I thought of all the wonderful times I had
Sitting in my mother's chair.
She must be worried,
Or maybe not.
I've gone 3 hours or more.
I turned around
Heard a small groan.
Looked over in horror
To see a small bird
Staggered and shaken with fear,
I cried a little cry,
Wiped my tears off.
Picked up the small bird,
And hurried quickly off.
I started to cry as my only company
Was this bird.
I slowly and firmly
Curled into a ball,
Making sure the bird was cool
Even though I was as hot as a burning fire.
So, now I suppose it's time to settle down,
And try not to feel sorry for myself.
Now all I can do is
Sleep, wish and hope someone comes.

Coleen MacDonald (11)
St James' Catholic High School, Colindale

I'VE NEVER HAD SO MUCH EXCITEMENT
IN MY ENTIRE LIFE

Stranded on a desert island,
What could possibly happen?
No parents,
Yippee!
I've never had the responsibility.
What fear?
There can't be anything out here.
Coconuts, pineapples,
What the hell?
I can eat them, without people saying,
That's enough you'll be ill.
I can relax,
Just sit and play,
Or just sleep all day,
No school,
No books,
No tellings-off,
No. 'That's enough play with your sister.'
So can't you see,
I'm as happy as can be.
I'm not missing home,
Not one tiny bit.
I'm not at school,
So I can say *writt*
Instead of write.
But you know I don't like night!
There's nothing really out here, is there?

Clare Casey (11)
St James' Catholic High School, Colindale

SHIPWRECK

As the boat began to rock from side to side,
I hit my head on the deck.
A hole became visible,
and water flowed in with great force and knocked me off my feet.
The waves hit up on the side of the boat as it started to sink.
I thought and jumped over the side of the boat but as I did
the man on the boat said, 'Man overboard.'
When the ship did sink I grabbed a piece of wood and started
to swim for an island I saw when I was on the ship.
On the island it was sticky.
I dried very quickly.
I looked around for some food and saw some fruit, grabbed it,
and started to eat it with great might.
When night came I started to get lonely, in the end I started
to get too hungry to write anymore.

Philip Morgan (12)
St James' Catholic High School, Colindale

HELP!

The island is the worst thing that could have
possibly happened to me,
It is hot and humid.
I am lonely and sad,
the birds attack you,
no one has passed by in days.
I have no food
apart from the unripened bananas hanging off the trees,
the monkeys eat them anyway.
I never thought I would say this but,
I miss my family and I want to go *home!*

Jenny Jackman (11)
St James' Catholic High School, Colindale

STUCK ON A DESERT ISLAND

D eserted on an island no way out,

E ndlessly struggling finding food.

S andy beaches splashing water.

E xcited but I feel like this is slaughter.

R ushing streams, dry rocks.

T ender leaves, and old docks.

E verlasting pineapple tree,

D ying animals, I'm going to die 'Help me'.

I sland's hot, island's sticky.

S un shining.

L aser beams on me.

A ching skin, *crash!* I fell with weakness.

N ever ending sound flowing in my head.

D eadly dying darkness, I will not go on again.

Elviae Casimir-Lascaris (11)
St James' Catholic High School, Colindale

SHIPWRECKED

D esert island, so lonely and afraid.

E ating coconuts day after day. Nothing to do,
but sitting in the sand is like a frying pan.

S hip after ship can't get help, they are sailing
past really fast.

E vening after evening sitting on the sandy beach,
sipping coconuts from the coconut tree.

R esting on my only companion, this tall coconut tree.

T ime is ticking no time for this spree I must start my journey
to find a good cup of tea.

Omar Henry (11)
St James' Catholic High School, Colindale

MY DESERT ISLAND THOUGHTS

Under the palm tree
I sit and stare
Wondering if I'll ever get out of here.

Why did my ship have to sink
Maybe if I hadn't been so bad.

When I was swimming in the deep blue sea
I suddenly remembered what I had seen;
A great big ugly thing.

My mum had always said to me
Never swim in a deep blue sea,
If you come across a sea creature
Never touch it,
Never scream.

Laura Hunter (11)
St James' Catholic High School, Colindale

DESERT ISLAND

The waves are splashing,
the boat is crashing.
We are all shouting 'Help, help'
endless on the shore.
We don't know what to do,
I hope we don't have to stay here anymore.
We are trying to get people's attention
by waving a flag around,
because I am afraid we are all going to drown.
We are never going to be saved
because all we do is wave a flag around.

Alexandra Hazel (12)
St James' Catholic High School, Colindale

THE DESERT ISLAND

Out in the sun
Is a lot of fun.
There were coconuts
And some broken huts.

All the palms
Had loads of arms.
Falling fruits
Were real brutes.

I was bored so I moaned,
And groaned.
I lay in the sun and my back ached,
So it started to bake.

Neil Jahans (11)
St James' Catholic High School, Colindale

THE DESERT ISLAND

The desert island I am on is very hot
I feel like I am being boiled in a witch's pot
I made a boat
But it did not float
I caught a fish and had it for my dish
I looked high in the sky
And saw a few birds fly by
I hear noises and think they are beasts
But that is the thing I want to see least
The trees are big and tall
I am afraid they will tumble and fall
I am always in the sun
And having loads of fun.

Lavinia Zecca (11)
St James' Catholic High School, Colindale

DESERT ISLAND

D esert island, what am I to do?
E verything is quiet and I'm feeling quite blue.
S earching for water and some type of life too.
E verlasting thirst lingers in my mouth and I'm not very cool.
R aging for a river or a little water pool,
T emperature is high and no place is cool.
E ach animal is as quiet as a mouse,
D istracted, and I wish I was in my house.

I see something scuttling and realise it is a louse,
S urprised it is here on a desert place like this.
L ifelessly, I crunch my fist,
A ll my memories come back to me, I remember when I last saw
     my mum and gave her a little kiss.
N ever have I ever missed my little cat,
D aily, I used to see her curled on her little mat.

Stacey Hunter (12)
St James' Catholic High School, Colindale

DESERT ISLAND

I was stranded on an island,
deserted and alone,
I didn't know what to do,
it was just me and the blue sea.
What would you do if it was you?

Here I am alone and sad,
sitting here with me and my tears,
I've been here for many a day.

I'm still here, me and my tears,
I don't know what to do,
I'm stuck here like glue.
I'm sad and alone with nothing else
but a bone.

I'm still here, I want to go soon,
but what can I do?
I could do more if it was two,
so bye for now I'll see you soon,
I'm here with no more than a spoon.

Rachael Smith (11)
St James' Catholic High School, Colindale

DESERT ISLAND

Splash wrrr goes the sea.
The waves crash and lash over the side.
Splash wham over I go into the Pacific Ocean.
Then I went blank and woke up
and found a plank and floated to desert island.
I felt sad, my head hurt bad.
I got up and walked and with no one I talked
because I was on a deserted desert island.
I found fresh water and gulped it all up
and then I fell down a 300 foot drop.
I landed in the sea, the fall almost killed me.
I wandered for days in the bright sun's haze,
eating little or no food.
One day by the beach I saw a boat
which had come to rescue me.
I jumped in the sea and swam to the boat,
climbed aboard, set sail and survived to tell the tale.

Gary Casey (11)
St James' Catholic High School, Colindale

ON A DESERT ISLAND

On a desert island,
alone and in a trance.
I looked around and all I could
see was palms and the
waves splashing upon the beach.
My thoughts drifted from me,
to the things that I love
best, my TV, radio and
even my best cassettes
I thought some more,
and gave a little sigh as I
remembered my family and
had a cry.
The things we take for
granted,
in every day we grow.
My day on the desert
island I now began to know.

Leanne Kenny (11)
St James' Catholic High School, Colindale

DESERTED

D angerous creatures are among you
E ating food that you don't know is poisonous.
S   ea monsters surrounding the island.
E verything is not safe on the island.
R escued by someone is just what I need.
T omorrow will be another day stranded on a deserted island.
E very day and every night I was scared.
D o I want to live or not?

Antonio Marcelino (11)
St James' Catholic High School, Colindale

TRAPPED ON AN ISLAND

Under the hot sun
Not having fun
Why did the boat have to sink?
I can't even think.

Lots of palm trees
I wonder will I have to pay my boat fees?
I remember when the ship sunk
Right now I wish I was in my bunk.

There is a beautiful waterfall
But there is no one to call
As I staggered onto the sand
I thought well at least I might get tanned.

That was one heck of a storm
God it is so warm
What a big volcano
I hope there won't be a tornado.

I got lost in the forest
But I found my pet dog Boris
Everywhere is as dry as a bone
I'm so alone.

I can't find my case
Will I ever leave this place?
I look every day for a boat -
If I don't see one soon I'll cut my throat.

Rory Leyne (11)
St James' Catholic High School, Colindale

DESERT ISLAND STRAND

This desert island is fun, exciting and scary,
I'm looking for shelter I hope I meet a fairy.
As I first woke up I was completely dry,
I wish I would be put out of my misery I'm sure
I'm going to shrivel up and die.
As I walk through and through along the desert's shore,
My feet dragging along the ground then it started to pour.
As I looked endlessly to find water I saw some shipmates,
As I walked closer to them the ground started to shake.
I shouted out 'Hold on tight,' they wouldn't listen to me
and faded away,
And the same thing happened the next day.
As I live alone on this desert island strand,
When I get home I am going to listen to an all-timer band.

Vincent Shailer-Dolan (12)
St James' Catholic High School, Colindale

DESERT ISLAND

D esert island,
E verywhere there is noise
S ome of the animals scare me
E arly in the morning I get up in search of food
R ivers, in the rivers there are fish
T he volcano is about to erupt

I solated, I am isolated
S oon I will die
L and is getting dehydrated
A nimals crowding round me
N ever will I leave this island, I might as well
D ie.

Christina Fitzgerald (11)
St James' Catholic High School, Colindale

WHAT IS THIS PLACE?

The storm was rough and heavy,
And threw the boat to and fro,
Splash, smash and crash went the waves,
It flung me off the boat.
I float.

I woke to find myself alone
In a place I never knew,
I felt so lonely, so deserted,
I was truly abandoned
I'm stranded.

I went in search of water,
My throat so dry, so crisp
Do I see a fountain?
No it's merely an illusion,
Delusion.

Evening is closing in,
I quest for shelter,
Will I find a tree hut,
Or will I only find sand?
What is that by the waves?
It's caves.

But will it be filled with danger?
A bear, wild animals or cavemen,
Cannibals could be lurking.
I try to find a place to hide,
Survive.

Joanne Mullins (11)
St James' Catholic High School, Colindale

DESERT ISLAND

On the desert island I walk in the calm breeze,
The loneliness I feel I can't describe.
The hot sun shining on my back,
As I lonely, walk through the deserted island.
I come across a rock,
I sit down to rest my aching legs.
I think of happy things to brighten up my day,
I listen to the bees buzzing around my head.
I also listen to the birds whistling a beautiful song,
I fall asleep, I dream about being with my friends and family.
I wake up, it's just a dream.
I sometimes wonder what's going on
in the world with people.
Although it's peaceful, I do miss my family.

Alice McGee (11)
St James' Catholic High School, Colindale

DESERTED ISLAND

D eserted island a land in space,
E verything's gone even the human race.
S and is everywhere,
E ven in my hair.
R aging for water
T o drink and to shave
E ndlessly I cannot find.
D oomed we're doomed, someone said from behind.

I 'm thinking, thinking what to do,
S o I come up with a plan for me and my crew.
L and is deserted and trees are dead,
A nd I think we should build a hut.
N ext we should make a fishing rod,
D one and finished now we can catch our fish.

Declan McCarthy (11)
St James' Catholic High School, Colindale

STRANDED

I'm stranded on an island
with beautiful palm trees.
I love the insect noises
and the sea, nice and calm
with smooth sand surround
and the sea, nice and calm, it stays calm forever,
and rocks and shells getting washed up on the shore
and the sea opens its doors waiting for more
as if a car is waiting for a drink of petrol.
Sandals slithering through the smooth sand
and crabs eating their prey
and saying it gets better every day.
Mountains lurking in the background.
Winds staying quiet not making a noise.
I want to go home now and to leave this ground.

Scott McNicholas (11)
St James' Catholic High School, Colindale

DESERTED

As I sat there on my own,
Wondering what they're doing at home,
Fear flowing through my mind,
Don't know what's gonna come up behind.

Swimming in the deep blue sea,
With red and green seaweed tangled beneath me.

As I swam in the deep blue sea,
I suddenly remembered what my mum told me.
Little sea creatures everywhere,
Better be careful, better beware.

As I stumbled on the slippery sand,
I fell down and rested my hands.
I shut my eyes and had a dream,
I dreamt that my mum came to rescue me.

Jemma Barry (11)
St James' Catholic High School, Colindale

DESERT ISLAND

Deserted place, must be an island,
I am sure I'll be home soon.
No one to talk to, nowhere to do my hair.
What if my friends heard about life over here?
I'm missing my friends and my family.
All I can talk to is a rock or a tree.
At least they don't argue back.
The sand is boiling hot, it hurts my feet,
But then I can jump into the nice cooling sea.

Rachel Slattery (11)
St James' Catholic High School, Colindale

DESERT ISLAND

Things are really weird I felt a lot of fear.
I looked around and saw a bush
it moved to a kind of dance groove,
I heard a noise it was very weird
then I saw a face with a blue beard.

Then at the dock just above the rock
I saw a boat with cheers and shouts.
It was very weird, it seemed to annoy
the bloke with a blue beard.
He ran away as if he was scared
then a tribe came out
when they saw the pirates
with a scream and shout they
all ran out.

I thought I was going to die, said I.
I ran and I ran when afloat.
I saw a boat lead by a goat.
It was really weird, he said
'Get on the boat which is afloat
and has a picture of a goat.'
I got on the boat with the goat
and back to England we sailed.

Daniel Llewellyn (11)
St James' Catholic High School, Colindale

DESERT ISLAND

One morning it was a sunny day,
On summer fields bay,
I couldn't hear any moans,
So we dug for dinosaur bones.

We couldn't leave,
I had sand up my sleeve.
The large ship made an awful noise,
And I could see plenty of boys.

The waves crashed off the edge of the sea,
And going round my head there was a bee.
There weren't many people there,
And I wasn't at all scared.

I waved for the ship to see me
But I don't think the driver could see,
It sailed straight past,
And the driver laughed.

The next day it was very cold,
And the sand was turning to mould.
The ship came again and I got on,
But the fee was a con.

Kate Tracey (11)
St James' Catholic High School, Colindale

A Blank Page

It is all I ever think about
The one thing on my mind
The thing that keeps on churning
Throughout the whole of my life.

Whenever I am thinking
I am thinking about it
Whenever I need any help at all
I get my help from it.

But this thing is private
It can never be spread around
So whenever people ask about it
I tell them it is a blank page.

A blank page
Deep within my mind.

Anneliese Clarke (12)
St Mary's CE High School, Hendon

What Is A Hamster?

What is a hamster?
Its head is as long as my thumb.
Its teeth are as sharp as a knife;
Its whiskers are like thin pieces of straw;
Its claws are like sticks coming from a branch;
In a cage slow and creepy;
Out of cage fast and scary.
At night it looks for its prey.
Happiness
Walks with it.

Kyle Alveran (11)
St Mary's CE High School, Hendon

MY HELPFUL BRAIN

My dear brain helps me in a lot of things,
It helps me to play, pray and work,
It helps me to sing, sleep and feel,
It makes me look, cook and loot,
And even helps me smell and hear.
It helps me to breathe,
And makes my teeth grow!
It helps me to walk, wake and work,
And even makes me cry and laugh.
It tells me when I'm hungry,
It tells me when I'm angry,
And reminds when it's time to play.
It asks me questions like,
'What's the time?'
'What's his name?'
Or 'How old is he?'
And even 'How much is that?'
So that's why I say,
My brain is helpful,
All the time.

Louis Mateega (12)
St Mary's CE High School, Hendon

ADULTS

Adults shout at you for the slightest thing.
When they shout at you it's like a bee sting.
They shout and they shout till the day is done.
At the end they make you feel like scum.

Adults, adults are everywhere.
Looking at you with a deadly stare.
As soon as you make the slightest mistake,
They come straight at you like a garden rake.

Adults are all over the streets,
Treating you like a cheap piece of meat.
When you're lacking a little post-haste,
They'll shout at you like a slap in the face.

One day I'll get them back,
I'll form a massive attack.
Till the day kids rule the world
I'm stuck here with adults at the age of twelve.

Ian Anoff (12)
St Mary's CE High School, Hendon

IT WAS ONE DAY

It was one day
I went to play
I kicked the ball up
high in the sky.
It nearly hit someone
who was very tall.
He freaked out and
gave a shout
'Who did that.'
It was that boy with
the red Arsenal hat,
said one man with a cat.
I said 'Sorry' hiding
behind a lorry. My friend
was scared, the man
said 'It doesn't matter.'
He crossed over on his
way to Dover. We said
'Goodbye' with a pie.

Chris McDonagh (12)
St Mary's CE High School, Hendon

LOST AND FOUND

I was helping my sister with homework
when my mother ran into the room.
'I've found it, I've found it, I've found it,' she cried
and then she sat down in gloom.
'I had it, I had it, I had it,' she frowned
the best thing I ever did see.
'What was it, what was it, what was it,' I cried
and then she stood and sighed, 'I cannot remember
precisely' she said 'but it was something beginning with *d*.'

'A dob or a dabble, a dish or the devil
a dog or a dart a dame or a damsel
a dancer with twenty left legs?' I asked.

'No none of those things, it was something more beautiful than them.'

'A diagnosis a dial a dialect or a diamond
a diary a diaper a dingo or a diploma
or a donkey with tiny little ears?' I proposed.

'No, no it's none of those, try again and again.'

' A dinosaur its dinner a dolly or a diver
a Doberman a doctor a dollar or a dolphin
a doob a domino a drum or a dormouse
your daddy you . . .'

'That's it' she cried, 'it's your new daddy whom I am to marry,
his name is Daniel D.'

Andreas Charalambous (12)
St Mary's CE High School, Hendon

THE GIRL NEXT DOOR

The girl next door is very, very sweet
and is very, very neat. She's tidy
and simple faced.

In the morning she wakes up to put
the rubbish out. And in 10 minutes
she is ready.

She has golden hair with crisp clean shoes
and her uniform is never in a mess
because she's the best and
when we're in school she's so cool.

She's cool, she's clean, she's the best
ever, ever. She sings, she plays,
and weighs six pounds. She's not
thin or too fat, just right. So the
girl next door is very, very sweet
and is very, very neat.

Priya Makwana (12)
St Mary's CE High School, Hendon

DOLPHINS

Its head is like a duck's head;
Its colour is blue,
Its fins are like triangles,
Its body is shaped like a knife,
Its skin is like a rainbow,
In the water it swims like a fish,
Landing in the water it is like a diver,
In the water it likes to play.

Carmine Mattia (11)
St Mary's CE High School, Hendon

KEY OF DESTRUCTION

Evil is the key to destruction, where there is no
key there is no knowledge.

There was one boy, a farmer's boy, who didn't
show hurt or play with any toys, he spent his
childhood as a chicken farmer and his name
was Zaina.

He grew up knowing no one loving or caring for anyone,
he wanted to learn more about the truth,
he past troubles and trials and yet he was confused,
he was the son of Vixen, but he passed away long ago,
who could tell him the truth . . .

but sometimes the truth leads to destruction.

Evil is similar to love, you can love the concept or hate it,
it's like an obsession, panting and wanting more of it.
Sometimes you can overcome,
but most times it overcomes you.

This also happened to that young Knight Zaina
he was bold and brave but later on in his life
thinking of his father's death made him lash out

at innocent men, women and children then because
the evil overcame him, he finally finished his life
with suicide, but he always remembered the saying
'Vengeance is in the eye of the beholder'.

Michael Campbell (12)
St Mary's CE High School, Hendon

THE POLAR BEAR

What is a polar bear?
Its body; a fluffy white cloud,
Its head a big white ball,
Its legs big strong weights,
Its arms are like a big roll of vanilla ice-cream.

Its size very big, like two tigers put together,
Its eyes are like two black marbles,
Its fur, very soft, like snow,
Its claws are like very sharp pencils,
Its ears, very powerful, just like a battery,
Its teeth, very sharp like elephant's tusks.

On the ground it's like a trotting horse,
When it's hunting it's like a sneaking snake,
When it eats, it eats like an elephant,
Walking on ice it becomes a flying bird,
Living on the ice, in the cold, it is like something
   that a human being can never do;
Pride walks with it.

Forum Shah (12)
St Mary's CE High School, Hendon

A TORTOISE IS?

A tortoise's shell is as hard as a roof of a house,
A tortoise's shell is as hard as a flat ball of steel.
A tortoise's head is as small as a microscopic cell.
Its eyes are as small as a full stop on a piece of writing.
A tortoise is as slow but bigger than a snail -
Most tortoises are herbivorous, they also eat but have no teeth.
A tortoise's shell is a semi-transparent shell of the hawksbill turtle.

Jahmai Turner (11)
St Mary's CE High School, Hendon

THE SEA SERPENT

It's 1341 on the seas of the cursed,
We can't drink this saltwater we have to thirst.
It's our last resting place the sea of the cursed,
The fumes and gases almost make our eyes burst.
These noxious gases may deceive us whilst in this hell,
Are those sharp teeth? Our poor eyes can't tell.
From the gates of Hades this monster rose its head,
Giving people nightmares whilst in bed.
Then it attacked us breathing fiery breath,
This beast is evil, it sides with death.
Again it breathes its fiery breath.
My crew die fighting, I alone escape,
I should have stayed to fight.
Now I'm nowhere, no land or light,
Trapped in my madness no help in sight.

Tunde Hazzan (13)
St Mary's CE High School, Hendon

HOMELESSNESS

H oping hungry the homeless people beg
O ver hills and through the polluted town
M oney problems haunt them for eternity
E mpathising I see them suffering, surviving through a winter's night
L ong journeys along an uneasy life
E mpty stomachs groan for food, as they beg for money
S ullen faces I see as I walk through the dark alleys
S hining street lights beam down on their skinny bodies
N eglected and ignored as they search for food
E nvious and depressed, with sympathy, I feel for them
S ick, ill, unsafe and unloved
S trange, unpleasant and unkind people just stroll past.

Velma Candy (12)
St Mary's CE High School, Hendon

THE ELEPHANT

What is an elephant?
Its head is like a big grey rock; it's body like a lorry;
Its trunk like a long, long worm; its ears like big leaves;
Its tusks are big sharp knives; its tail, a short rope;
Its feet like an earthquake; its weight like a mountain;
It's high like the skyscrapers and its colour like the sky before the rain.

The elephants are vegetarians, with their trunk
they can take down an entire tree!
The elephants move slowly, very slowly
because they are so heavy.
They live in the deep jungles of India and Africa.
The noise that the elephant makes is like a trumpet!

Hagar-Iron (12)
St Mary's CE High School, Hendon

MY BEST BIRTHDAY EVER

My best birthday was when I was ten
'Growing up' said all my friends.

I laughed and played in the park,
time to go it's getting dark.

Jelly, ice-cream, apple pie time to go
say goodbye.

Hugs and kisses here and there
'Bye Shamaine' everywhere.

Now I'm alone on my own nobody's home
I'm on my own.

Shamaine Boyce (12)
St Mary's CE High School, Hendon

WHAT IS A ZEBRA?

Its head is like a black and white camouflaged picture.

Its feet are like a slab of steel.

Its tail is like a bunch of rough hair on a paint brush.

Its movement is like a bird flying through thin air.

Its eyes are like glittering stars.

Its ears are like a cuddly bear's ears.

Its body is as firm as a wooden table.

Its size is just like a horse's size.

Their climate is as hot as a baking oven.

Their habitat is as quiet as a silent room.

The water they drink is as soft as raindrops.

Their enemies are as fierce as lions.

Its hearing is as accurate as a scale.

When crouching while sleeping is like a prowling leopard.

Pride walks with it.

Karina Roseway (11)
St Mary's CE High School, Hendon

WHAT IS A COCKATOO!

Its head is like a yellow furry ball,
Its eyes are like small black balls.
Its body is as bright as the sun,
Its claws are like eagle's but smaller,
Its wings are like small yellow, feathery tubes.

In flight it glides past the sun, glittering on its way;
On the ground it plays, climbs and moves,
Just like a swift dancer.
When it is sleeping it is as quiet as a mouse,
and when it's awake it's as noisy as elephants.
Cute walks with it.

Carla Powell (11)
St Mary's CE High School, Hendon

MAD ABOUT HEALTH

I eat carrots,
I eat cabbage,
I eat sprouts,
I eat radish.

Don't eat sugar,
Don't eat fat,
What about salt,
Don't eat that.

Look after myself,
I'm mad about health,
Mad about health,
Mad about myself.

I go for a jog,
I go for a swim,
I go for a run,
I go to the gym.

I got the gear,
I got the kit,
Got the shoes,
It's a perfect fit.

Minal Wadhia (11)
St Mary's CE High School, Hendon

ONCE HE SPOTS YOU . . .

What is a blue shark?
Its body is like a big fish,
With a length of 3 metres
And its teeth look like blades in a row,
People say there he goes,
When he is hunting for his prey:
He has five gill slits in a row,
That look like lollipop sticks you know;
His skin is smooth like silk,
If you touch he might go munch.

He sways side to side,
As he looks for his prey,
Oh no the prey tries swimming away,
But it's not their day
Because he is amongst the most voracious
Of all predatory fish.
So once he spots you,
There is one thing to say . . .

>   *It's your*
>   *Doom!*

Nicole Bandoo (11)
St Mary's CE High School, Hendon

WHAT IS A PANDA?

A panda's head is like a black and white football,
Its chest is as furry as a gorilla,
Its claws are like sharp nails,
There is only a few and they're always being
hunted down and used for clothes.
It's bigger and tougher than a gorilla,
You can get them in large and small sizes.

It quietly moves, searching for its food,
It sits there munching its bamboo shoots,
They love rolling around in the grass and
like playing with their friends.
On the ground they make their babies by birth,
Extinction walks with it.

Jonathan Norton (11)
St Mary's CE High School, Hendon

ARSENAL

Arsenal, the king of kings,
Arsenal, always winning the honours.
Arsenal, showing glitz, glamour and goals.
Whether it is the women's team,
Or whether it is the men's team,
They've always entertained me so,
I will always stick beside them.
Alex Manninger or David Seaman,
Martin Keown or Tony Adams,
Giles Grimandi or Lee Dixon,
For me, they are all a sensation.
Emmanuel Petit or Patrick Viera,
Marc Overmars or Ray Parlour,
Dennis Bergkamp or Ian Wright,
Showing genius football and putting up a good fight.
The speed and the pure class of
Nicholas Anelka and Christopher Wreh,
Well, what can I say?
Brilliant footballers and eye catching skills,
Giving me and our supporters brilliant thrills.

Panish Patel (13)
St Mary's CE High School, Hendon

YOUR BEST MATE

When things get too rough
And the going gets tough
Your mum's moaning
You dad's groaning
Just remember one thing
Give your best mate a ring.

Chat about this,
Chat about that,
Then you'll remember one thing
I'm glad I gave my best mate a ring!

Your room's a mess,
You're suffering from stress
You've got loads of homework to do,
You think you're coming down with the flu
Just remember one thing
You've already gave . . .
Your best mate a ring!

Sharon Yemoh (13)
St Mary's CE High School, Hendon

MY HERO

My hero is my dad.
He is the strongest man in the world.
He works all day and helps me with my homework.
But most of all when I have a football match,
he always tells me to do my best and that is all.
So at the end of the day I know my dad loves me
and he knows I love him.

Akif Mehmet (12)
St Mary's CE High School, Hendon

POLLUTION

People destroy this beautiful world,
Others try to stop them,
Litter is one of the worst forms of pollution,
You should always recycle,
The ozone layer is being destroyed,
If everyone polluted we would be living in a dump,
Oh please don't litter this world,
Now we have the chance to clean up this world!

We shouldn't drive cars that run on petrol,
It sends off gases into the universe,
If you keep on destroying the ozone layer,
There will be flash floods,
Most people will drown in the flood.

Kieren Russell (12)
St Mary's CE High School, Hendon

MY COMPUTERS

One day I got a computer, it was a Sega Mega-drive.
I had lots of games for it, 29 for show
My sister Lana used to play with me
Until it broke after tea
One year later I got another
After conferring with my mother
When my sister Marina played, she was so bad
But my sister Lana was so fab
I still have my PlayStation to this day
18 games I play all day
With Time Crisis I can't keep away
But now I've got a Pacard Bell PC
I don't play as much, it's such a pity!

Gabriel Gutierrez (12)
St Mary's CE High School, Hendon

ALIEN FROM MARS

I met an orange alien with a long pink nose
His teeth were purple and arranged in rows.
He comes from Mars where blue grass grows,
He has fourteen legs and fifty-two toes.

This alien I met has a big round head,
And every ten days is when he gets fed.
Every ten hours he goes to bed,
Then gets up to search for his food again.

Now it's time for me to go home,
In my small rocket all alone.
I wonder if I'll meet their alien again,
Who felt to me he had no friend.

Elakeche Ella (13)
St Mary's CE High School, Hendon

THE SNAKE

What is a snake?
A snake's skin is as scaly as a lizard's head,
Its tongue is like a fork end,
Its head is like a pen's end,
Its body, shaped like the letters,
Its belly is like a baby's bottom.

It lives in the desert, on the warm soft sand,
It slithers in the shape of the letter 'S',
Its hiss is like the sound a gas cooker makes,
It moves sideways like a crab,
It leaves Sssss on the ground,
Pride slithers with it.

Lamarr Douglas (11)
St Mary's CE High School, Hendon

WHERE TO GO

Where to go, where to go, I just don't know where to go.
Cyprus, Asia, Peru or Rome I just can't think where to go.
Maybe a place in California, Paris, Athens or Carolina,
An island in the Isle of Man or maybe I'll go to Milan.
We could go to Pompeii, see the volcanoes one day,
China, Japan, I just don't know!
Where do you think I should go?
No, no I'm not going there I really do not like Bell-Air,
Everyone aboard just always stare, stare, stare.
Kenya, yes I'll go to Kenya.
Hear the stories they can tell.
But I'm short of cash,
I'll just go to Devon,
Caravans are nice.
Beach is lovely,
But the best thing is the ice-cream shop next door!

Neil Bennett (12)
St Mary's CE High School, Hendon

WHAT IS A PANDA?

Its head, a big balloon, its neck, a big trunk of wood,
Its body, a small black and white cloud.

His claws like a small sharp knife,
Its nose like a round wet bouncy ball,
When he plays, he rolls through the grass,
Like a pig in the mud.

Walking, it becomes a leopard looking for his prey.
Cute walks with it.

Daniela Holguin (11)
St Mary's CE High School, Hendon

THE MAN NEXT DOOR

The man next door has a small brown back door it looks like a flat
rat in one way.
The man next door has a flat black cat which looks like the front
door mat.
The man next door has a blue van which looks like a can and he
calls it Dan.
The man next door has a car which can't go far.
He has a dog which looks like a log.
The man next door has a red and blue rickshaw near the front door.
The man next door has a green living room floor which goes up
to the door.
He has a purple door which doesn't match the floor.
The man next door always hangs on the door because he is scared
of the floor.
One day the man next door went somewhere and never came back
so there I don't care.

Charitha Jayatilaka (13)
St Mary's CE High School, Hendon

WHAT IS A TIGER?

What is a tiger?
Its teeth as sharp as the tip of a knife,
Its claws, shaped like a dinosaur's toenail,
Its head, scarier than Godzilla,
Its skin, as smooth as a cat
Its foot, perching towards its prey,
When it's hunting it's like a meteorite striking Earth,
Ferocity walks with it.

Nicky Wong (11)
St Mary's CE High School, Hendon

AUTUMN AGAIN

Gloomy autumn has come
again.
Summer has gone no more
Spain.
The sky is dull with mist
and rain
and now we're back to school
again.

The leaves so gold floating
on air.
The sky so bold with clouds
so fair.

Autumn is now beginning
again.
So autumn good morning
and
Summer good night.

Lavina Suthenthiran (12)
St Mary's CE High School, Hendon

WHAT IS A PIG?

Its legs are like a ruler,
Its tail is like a piece of ribbon being tied on a parcel,
Its snout is like the end of a cotton reel,
Its stomach is like a big ball,
It eats like a race is on,
When it gets down and rolls around
It ends up like a pile of mud.

Siân Saxton (12)
St Mary's CE High School, Hendon

NIGHTMARE

There's something under my bed.
I've always known it was there, ever since I was little.
Mum thinks it's just in my head.
Parents don't know anything. Then again, they're always right . . .
but what if it gets me in the middle of the night?
Two glowing eyes, that's all I see of it.
I know it's there, hiding in the gloom.

Waiting,
Watching
In the corner of my room.

Now it's dark again. What should I do?
I switch on my torch, but the batteries are up.
I reach for the lamp, but there's been a power cut.
The darkness closes in on me.

And I know that the *something* under my bed is still
waiting patiently.
I have to get rid of it!
There's only one way . . .

Slowly, quietly, I get out of bed.
I look underneath to see what's there . . .

And all that I find is a glowing teddy bear!

Dilan Kanli (13)
St Mary's CE High School, Hendon

THE CAT

Its head is as small as a tennis ball,
Its paw is smaller than a lion's claw,
Its tail is as long as a rope,
Its whiskers are as thin as a piece of thread,
Its nose is the shape of a heart,
Its teeth are as sharp as a butcher's knife.

Sometimes the cat moves slow,
Sometimes the cat moves fast,
The cat can run like a human on all fours,
The cat can run like the wind,
The cat can leap like it's in the Olympics,
The cat needs its sleep because it gets tired very easily.

Manisha Sahni (11)
St Mary's CE High School, Hendon

WHAT IS A GIRAFFE?

Its head is like a big shoe,
Its neck is like a long, thick rope,
Its ears are like a soft cloud,
Its skin is like a giant leopard,
Its eyes are like small bouncy balls,
Its feet are lady's high clogs.

It moves like a trotting horse,
Its feet move like a galloping horse,
It walks across the grass peacefully,
Its children playing happily, pouncing, running,
Leaping and jumping all over the place.

Vanetta Richards-Lindo (11)
St Mary's CE High School, Hendon

WHAT IS A KILLER WHALE?

Its fins are as sharp as a knife,
Its teeth are like a butcher's knife,
Its tongue is slippery like a slithering snake,
Its jaws are like an animal foot trap,
It eats like a 100 lions eating a man,
Its skin colour is like a zebra crossing,
It glides though the water like a bird flying
through the sky
It dives like a dolphin,
Its bones are as flexible as a piece of paper bending,
It's as fast as a torpedo going through the water.

Ramvir Singh Padam (11)
St Mary's CE High School, Hendon

THEIR WAY

Suiting, smiling, styling,
Why?
Because it's their way.
Waking up, breaking up, making up,
Why?
Because it's their way.
Crazy, hazy, lazy,
Why?
Because it's their way.

Motivation, imagination, celebration,
Why?
Because it's *my way!*

Joanne Lindsay (13)
St Mary's CE High School, Hendon

ARSENAL

Arsenal are The Gunners,
We win every match we play,
We knock down all in our path,
So you'd better move out of our way!
We're better than Leeds United,
We're better than Chelsea too,
We're superior to Liverpool,
And we totally thrash Man U!
We've got Bergkamp and Anelka,
Who always hits the back of the net,
Parlour and Overmars on the wings,
Whatever will we think of next!
Petit and Viera play midfield,
And the famous four at the back,
Safe hands Seaman and cap'n Adams,
We're the best and that's a fact!
Adams, Dixon, Winterburn,
Seaman, Ljundberg, Vivas too,
Bould and Keown in defence,
Winnin' is what they do!
The back four carry on,
Year after year after year,
Defying their ages and critics,
Bringing up the rear!
Arsenal, they rule football,
Because they are the best,
I don't care what people say,
'Cause they're far much better than the rest!

Michelle Burgess (13)
St Mary's CE High School, Hendon

Colours

Red   is for fear, anger and blood,
         sometimes red is the colour for love.

Orange is the sweet citrus fruit,
         it's bright and not dull, like the brown of plant roots.

Yellow is the sun, shining with joy,
         as it shines upon us you can tell it's not coy.

Blue   is the sea, reckless and wild,
         the source for all life, the Great River Nile.

Green   is the grass, lush and bright,
         the wide open fields, the home of field mice.

Indigo is a sapphire, a shimmering gem,
         the blue precious stone, a gift for your friends.

Colours, colours are here and there,
Colours, colours are everywhere.

Janet Wong (14)
St Mary's CE High School, Hendon

My Dream

My dream is to be the world's greatest footballer,
My dream is for everyone in the world to be treated with equal rights,
My dream is for everyone in my family to stay healthy and well,
My dream is to win the Lottery,
My dream is to win the World Cup,
My dream is to travel all around the world.

Richard Coker (12)
St Mary's CE High School, Hendon

NOTHING

The Nothingness was as silent as the slowly revolving moon,
The Nothingness was floating like a helium balloon,
Hanging in the air with a strong feeling of doom,
The Nothingness would conquer and the Earth surrender soon.

The Nothingness knew nothing of the threat it would impose,
It clung to the people like a heart drawn to a rose,
The lucid situation was a puzzle to the mind,
And the Nothingness stole courage which the people had to find.

The Nothingness so far away yet still it was so near,
The Nothingness would take over and Earth would disappear,
We cry because we took for granted precious yesteryear,
And the people would watch in silence as the world sheds its last tear.

The Nothingness was created by the darkest, saddest space,
The Nothingness came from nowhere and it came without a face,
Its purpose was to eliminate every single girl and boy,
And the burning, raging fire inside it was set on trying to destroy.

Susannah Sweetman (13)
St Mary's CE High School, Hendon

MR HALL

Mr Hall
Is certainly very small.
A mouse could eat him,
Hair and all.

Mr Mad
Is certainly bad,
And sometimes
He's even sad.

Reshma Patel (11)
St Mary's CE High School, Hendon

I CAN'T FIND YOU

Where are you, I can't find you?
I keep searching for you,
Everywhere I look you are not there,
I need you, I can't live without you,
Please let me find you, let me see your smile.

Let me hear your laugh,
Let me hear your voice again,
Please, where have you gone?
I feel alone, like a part of me is missing.

It feels like I'll never find you again,
Everyone says I have to say goodbye,
I should stop holding on to you,
Please come back.

I feel like I'm in a wood, it's raining,
I look behind every tree, every bush,
But you're not there, I see a cave,
I go in, hoping you're there,
But you're not.

I keep searching, but no, I don't think I will find you,
I hear a voice, it says I shouldn't be sad anymore,
That you've gone to a place where you see your family
Who have gone, past away.

It says that one day, everybody will go there,
I hope so, but it also says,
Stop searching, because I'll see you again,
In a place called Heaven.

It says there is a special someone there who is always with you,
And wherever I go the special someone will follow,
And when I go to Heaven I will see you.

I'm not sad anymore, but happy, now I know you've gone,
To a good place.

Catharine Bishop (12)
St Mary's CE High School, Hendon

AEROPLANES, AEROPLANES

Aeroplanes, Aeroplanes,
High in the sky,
Their engines roaring
As they go by.

As people and children get off the plane,
The pilot says to them 'Come again.'
The plane is so big, it should be called
'The Great Dane'.

When you're in the air the pilot calls,
'We are entering into turbulence
Fasten your seat-belts,
We're in for a rough ride.'

When the food is served
And the TV is on,
When you're in an aeroplane,
You can't go wrong.

High in the sky,
Don't look down!
You might get sick,
I hope your paper bag is thick.

Jermaine Raymond (14)
St Mary's CE High School, Hendon

WINTER

Winter is cold,
Winter is rough,
The sky is grey and seems very dull.
It rains heavily all day and night,
We're wrapped up in our beds all cosy and tight.
It's so cold!
Christmas comes every year,
It's such fun!
We get presents and cards of different colours and sizes.
Santa comes down our chimney to fill our
stockings with a whole load of stuff.
The Christmas tree shining as bright as a light.
Oh, it's exciting!
It snows in December and we get to play outside to make snowmen.
We make big, round snowballs and throw them at each other;
It's so hilarious!
So Christmas is gone and winter is gone,
And I'll be looking forward to seeing you
next year for a whole load of fun.

Sadia Dhakam (13)
St Mary's CE High School, Hendon

ST MARY'S AND MY FRIENDS

St Mary's School is really cool,
But it could be better with a swimming pool,
Hitesh, my friend, is good at yo-yo,
He did a trick that I don't know.
I have another friend called Paul Shaw,
But that's not all, I have many more.

Keith Clarke (12)
St Mary's CE High School, Hendon

MOVIE STAR

I wish I was a movie star,
all glamorous and posh.
I'd stay all night at fancy clubs,
and not worry about the dosh.

I'd meet all types of famous people,
on the movie sets,
Tom Cruise, Jim Carrey, Arnold Schwarznegger,
or even Kate Winslet.

And if the directors were too bossy,
and also a pain in the neck,
I could afford to have them sacked,
and still get a huge pay cheque.

If I got nominated for best actress,
in the Academy Awards,
I'd make sure I had the perfect dress
to collect the gleaming reward.

In my gracious acceptance speech,
I would thank producers and my aunty Grace,
And make sure for a finishing touch,
a tear of happiness would run down my face.

Amanda Rashid (13)
St Mary's CE High School, Hendon

PEOPLE OF THE RAINBOW

I'm gonna tell you about a rainbow,
a very special one,
sit back and enjoy
the poem has just begun.

Look at the clouds up in the sky,
glistening, shining way up high,
beyond those clouds is a bright rainbow,
Can you see it? Can you see it? Watch it glow.

Red is for the people,
that are not with us today.
Yellow is for the blind people,
lift up your hands and pray.
Pink is for the deaf people,
give them love to hear.
Green is for everyone, show them that you care.

Purple is for the good people,
forgive them of their sins.
Orange is for the bad people,
open their hearts and let God in.
Blue is for all of these people, the people of the rainbow.

Julian Douglas (13)
St Mary's CE High School, Hendon

CATS SLEEP

Cats sleep anywhere, on a table,
on a chair, in your hat, on your bed.
They even sleep on the window ledge,
cats sleep anywhere, any place,
they don't care.

Robert Mitchell (11)
St Mary's CE High School, Hendon

FOOTBALL

Football, the greatest game on Earth,
Believe it or not, even in places like Perth.
Football is about teamwork and skill,
Not about lack of effort and taking pills.

If you're a striker, you need to be a good shooter,
And if you're a defender, you need to be a good booter.
If you're a midfielder, you need to be skilful,
And if you're a goalie you need to be graceful.

Football is about getting goals,
Not about doing dirty fouls.
Football players have big hearts,
Also they are very smart.

Hitesh Kothari (13)
St Mary's CE High School, Hendon

FASHION VICTIM

Oh my god it's 6 o'clock,
Only two hours to go,
Till I go out I mean,
What shall I wear?
And what about my hair?
My make-up's a mess,
Should I wear the purple dress?
What shoes should I wear?
Maybe the blue pair.
Never mind, I'll just wear the purple dress, blue shoes,
My hair will do down, and my make-up's fine.
Oh well, I'm ready, love you and leave you.

Kate Marshall (13)
St Mary's CE High School, Hendon

DREAMS

As you become sleepy and day becomes night,
You feel kind of tired and turn off the light.
On your way back you bump your head,
But then you crawl back into bed.

You dream about the things you like,
You dream about that brand new bike.
You finally reach school on time,
You're a detective and you solve a crime.

But always remember and always beware,
At any time a dream can turn into a nightmare.

You dream you get one hundred on your test,
You dream you're better than the rest.
You dream that you are simply supreme,
You really must love this dream!

But always remember and always beware,
At any time a dream can turn into a nightmare.

You've had this dream all night long,
Oh my goodness, something's gone wrong.
Everything's gone, there must be a mistake,
What's that bright colour? Oh no, I'm awake!

But never the less you had no fear,
That's why your dream was a nightmare.

Steven Gayle (13)
St Mary's CE High School, Hendon

BIRTHDAY

It's my birthday today,
And I'm 9,
I'm having a party tonight,
And we'll play on the lawn
If it's fine,
There'll be John, Dick and Jim,
And Alan and Tim,
And Dennis and Brian and Hugh,
But the star of the show
You'll be sorry to know,
Will be Sue,
(She's my sister aged two,
And she'll yell till she's blue
In the face and be sick.)

Josephine Balfour (11)
St Mary's CE High School, Hendon

CANDLES

I see a candle
Lighted brightly
A white tube of wax
Melting slowly
Dribbling down
Flames different colours
Flickering left to right
Along comes wind
Black smoke rises
Away in the atmosphere
All that's left
Is a dead candle.

Shenalee Patel (12)
St Mary's CE High School, Hendon

THE SCUBA DIVE

1, 2, 3, dive! Bubbles rush down my wetsuit,
the water clears and fish swim in shoals
of silver, schools of minnows glide in
and out of the current, showing
off their shimmering scales.
Down among the coral beds,
parrot fish rub their heads on rocks,
and rays bounce over my head like
playful puppies. I flatten myself
against a rock as a lionfish passes by,
dolphins squeal and whales cry
and every minute a crab scuttles by.
Oh I think I like staying dry, so
I'll bounce up to the warmth and sunlight.

Jessica Ward (11)
St Mary's CE High School, Hendon

THE PLAGUE

In the village of Eyam, a long time ago,
There was a tailor who had a big blow
He soon found out a flee team was about,
He said, 'Hey, town stay together.'

As soon as people heard, they fled like birds,
But the people who were ill had to stay still,
People crying, people sad,
Nothing they could do but wait till they flew out.

It past, maybe a year or two,
Finally it was dying,
And wines started popping.

Amir Pourdanay (11)
St Mary's CE High School, Hendon

THE WITCHES' SPELL

The witches have a gruesome spell to show
How to make a cat and rat so fat,
Every spell has a price to pay.

Witches, witches go away,
It will be cold at night,
Till the clock strikes nine
Children will grow fat and dumb,
They even make your spells go dumb,
They'll have your necks crushed to death till
Someone has blood on your bed.

Spell, spell come to me,
Place the spell on you and me.
Every spell will make you remember,
There's a price to pay,
Let the witches be all dead, until the night
Leaks away.

Komal Patel (12)
St Mary's CE High School, Hendon

FOOTBALL

Football, we play it on and off the pitch.
We can play it on grass or on concrete.
You can play it in the rain, sun or in the snow.
I like football because it's fast, active and full of fun.
Practice your skills like dribbling, passing and shooting.
Attack and defence are tactics you need
to be a good footballer and to succeed.
Listen to me, don't lean on that fence,
get out, play football, you know that makes sense.

Aidan Nolan (11)
St Mary's CE High School, Hendon

MANCHESTER UNITED

I like to play football a lot,
My favourite team is Man U,
I like to watch them play,
But I love to see them score.

I think they're great in the International,
And super in the league.
They play with pride and passion,
And they're strong up front where they score.

I think their team is the best,
And a bit snazzier than the rest,
With their ability to run up the pitch
And score a free kick.

I hate it when they let in a goal,
I curse it when they do,
Especially when they lose.

Karl Martin (13)
St Mary's CE High School, Hendon

MICHAEL OWEN

Michael Owen he's such a star in front
of the goal he'll make his mark.
He takes a shot, the ball goes in, it's guaranteed
his team will win.
Young Michael Owen he's not even twenty and
we have seen him, he scores plenty.
His pace is frightening, you've seen him run
he's like a bullet out of a gun.
90 minutes are up and the whistle has blown
and that is my poem about Michael Owen.

Kieran Wilkinson (11)
St Mary's CE High School, Hendon

MY BED'S A SILVER SPACESHIP

When I wake up some mornings,
Not all is what it seems,
I drift in a land of make-believe,
Between real life and my dreams.

Strange creatures from the stories
That I read the night before,
Crowd in upon my drowsiness,
Through imagination's door.

Where sleep and waking overlap,
The alarm clock's jangling cry,
Is a roaring fire-tailed rocket,
Hurtling through the sky.

My bed's a silver spaceship,
Which I pilot all alone,
Whispering through endless atmospheres
Towards planets still unknown.

Ricardo Reittie (11)
St Mary's CE High School, Hendon

SPURS AT PRIDE PARK

Spurs met Derby at Pride Park
George Graham's first match but not in charge yet
It was a thriller
A real whizzer
Paulo Wanchope missed a sitter
David Ginola whizzed and did glitter
It was a corner!
And Sol Campbell headered it in and scored
Spurs 1 - Derby 0 was the final score.

Jason Case (12)
St Mary's CE High School, Hendon

ARE YOU SURE?

Are you sure that you want to open that door?
And see what's through that dark creaky door.
Then see that dark ugly face sitting on the floor,
Staring at you,
Pointing at you,
Screaming at you.
As you open the door the wind has a nasty howl to
it saying, *stop!*
The lightning strikes,
The thunder pounds down,
You *don't* want to open that nasty door.

Are you sure you want to open that door?
And see what's through that pretty door,
Then see a pretty angel sitting on the floor,
Smiling at you,
Talking to you,
Saying hello.
As you open the door, a pretty beam shines and
flowers fall from the ceiling,
The sun shines,
The birds sing,
You *do* want to open that pretty door.

Andrea Carr (12)
St Mary's CE High School, Hendon

Food

Chicken and rice is very nice,
Don't forget the spice.
Salt fish and dumplings,
Don't forget the plantain.
Full I feel,
After that big meal.
For dessert I had some jelly,
After that I switch on the telly.
I was feeling peckish in the night,
I thought I had stepped on my cat and it gave me a fright.
So I went to bed and banged my head,
My cat started to lick me because it thought I was dead!

Nelson Simon (12)
St Mary's CE High School, Hendon

Three Little Tigers

Three little tigers,
Jumping around the moon,
One jumped too far and landed on a baboon.

Two little tigers lying in a tree,
One fell out and broke his knee.

One little tiger,
Running through the woods,
The hunter shot him,
And he was gone for good.

Darren Zanre (12)
St Mary's CE High School, Hendon

MY BAD DAY

Woke up in the morning, hit my head,
Walked down the stairs, no dropped instead,
Got my breakfast, dropped my plate,
Never thought I was going to get burned as well.
Got out the door,
Thought I was going to be alright,
Dropped on the kerb, almost broke my leg.
Hopped on the bus,
The bus was packed,
I was squashed together,
I couldn't get out.
Got off the bus, caught my breath,
Looked at my watch,
Oh no I'm late.
Finally got into school, sat down,
Looked left and right,
There was no one around.
Someone came in said, 'What are you doing?'
I said, 'I'm here for school'
He said, 'It is Saturday morning!'

Francine Leach (12)
St Mary's CE High School, Hendon

CHRISTMAS

It is that time of year
Christmas just around the corner
Buying the turkey for the family
Which one to buy, small, medium or extra large
Is he going to give me any presents
The Christmas tree and decorations are up
All the waiting is over
Almost the end of this year.

Patrick Edgcumbe (12)
St Mary's CE High School, Hendon

LIFE'S A JOURNEY

Life's a journey,
A journey we take step by step,
Day by day,
During it, you make mistakes you regret,
And promises you can't keep.
Every day to wonder,
What's going to happen next in my life,
But you will never know.
Life brings sorrow, pain,
Happiness and joy to all.
We seek ahead of us, working hard,
But never knowing what's to happen.
Life's nothing but a dream,
It goes without control,
And when it is time,
The dream is no more.

Alpa Patel (14)
The Swaminarayan School

MY TRUE LOVE

Words cannot describe him
How much I miss him
I love him loads

I look up at the sky
Then I cry.
I ask God, why?
Why did such a good
Man have to die?
Why I am left here
Alone
Confused and scared.

I know he has gone
One step higher
But that won't make
My pain go away.

I wrote this poem
Especially for you
To show my love
Towards you.

Hinal V Patel (13)
The Swaminarayan School

TITANIC

We were on our way to America,
In the middle of the Atlantic,
An iceberg coming right our way,
Nothing else to say.

The Captain said the ship would sink,
Most people did not know,
They started finding out quite soon,
But could not see the moon.

Water began to enter the ship,
The doors began to close,
Some people started to drown,
And others began to frown.

The unsinkable Titanic began to sink,
And suddenly split in half,
Two hours went by very fast,
Titanic was in the past.

Shirel Patel (12)
The Swaminarayan School

YOUR OWN FLESH AND BLOOD

What you don't know is what you're afraid of,
And I'm afraid of it too,
But can I never talk to you again?
There's a part of me that wants to call you up
And talk to you as a friend
And there's a part of me that just wants to shut you *out!*
How can we be enemies?
When we have the same flesh and blood
What does it take to make your heart bleed?
You can get through,
There's nothing stopping you.
Nothing can take the fact
That we're only flesh and blood,
For years I've been following your case
And now is the first time I see your face.
I want to make you laugh,
And I want a chance to know you better
I'm just like you remember!
I'm a part of you
And I'm your own flesh and blood.

Banshree Pindoria (11)
The Swaminarayan School

LOVE

In this world, love is scarce
And when I see your face
My face trembles, my knees go weak
If only I could show my affection
Then you'd know how much I love you.

The day we went to the fair
I cherish the bear that you won
Now a month apart,
I want you near my sight
I cherish every kiss, every sigh that you gave.

All I want to say,
Is, come back to stay
'Cause, I . . . love . . . you.

Pooja Kanabar (15)
The Swaminarayan School

THE MOON

The moon is a white golf ball floating through the air.
It is a grey air balloon in the dark of the night.
It is a football in the back of a net.
The moon is a clock hanging on a black wall.
It is a light at the end of the tunnel.
It is a marble orbiting around in space.
It is a snowball being thrown.
The moon, it is a reflection of the sun.

Bhavin Patel (14)
The Swaminarayan School

FLIGHT

Somewhere, beyond the harsh reality of life,
there is a place that no man sees.
The birds, so free on wing, are flying - there
into the clouds.

Upwards, I see them soar into the blue.
With tears I watch them fly from sight,
leaving behind all cares for man to bear.
I am alone.

Heavenward, I gaze into the hazy empty space.
You know the way to peace and love.
Oh birds, when you go to paradise again,
take me with you.

Rohini Patel (15)
The Swaminarayan School

THE CRASH

On a cold icy November morning
As I was getting out of bed yawning
The peace was broken by the screeching of brakes
Which was followed by the scattering of crates
Everywhere on the road was broken glass
As a milk float was overturned by a Mercedes E-class
In the distance could be seen a blue flashing light
As a wailing white ambulance came to sight
Two green men ran out with a stretcher
To help the unlucky get better
Unfortunately the person was already dead
And was ready for his burial bed.

Ravi Ghodasara (13)
The Swaminarayan School

THE BIRD

It glided through the sky,
Zoomed through the air,
And passed by the other birds,
It sat there gallantly and superior amongst
the other common birds.

Birds flocked apart as the rightful worthy of
entity came through,
Food was captured, killed and served to this earth-shaking
individual,
It seemed it was respected and honoured by the others,
The birds fought amongst themselves over the distinct one,
Then a loud squawk came out,
And the birds froze,
Then fleetingly lifted off and flew with the wind.

Dharmesh Pankhania (15)
The Swaminarayan School

PEOPLE

I love the way he talks
I love the way he acts
I love the way he thinks about me
I love his smooth tendered skin

I hate the way he gets in trouble
I hate the way he fights with his friends
I hate the way they fall out
I hate the way they never talk

I love the way he thinks of me
I love the way he smiles
I love the way he says 'Hi'

I hate the way he's never there
I hate the way he hugs and says 'Bye'
I hate it when his eyes don't shine on the sun.

Priya Kerai (12)
The Swaminarayan School

THE WOODS

Green, orange, red and brown,
That's all I see.
I am walking through the misty woods,
Trying to find a wooden house.
All I hear is the whistling wind
And the cracking of leaves, twigs and sticks.

The sky turns grey to black,
Suddenly I see eyes like I have never seen before,
Yellow, red, white and black,
What should I do, run or keep on walking?

The clouds start to move in,
Suddenly the clouds block the moon,
It's dark, I cannot see anything,
I am not scared I keep telling myself,
I keep on walking.

Suddenly, *bang, bang,*
I start to run,
I find a door,
I wonder should I go in or should I not go in?
Then I run in and . . .

Alopi Patel (14)
The Swaminarayan School

MOTHER'S LOVE

Without my mother I wouldn't be here today,
I wouldn't be in the soft, gentle arms
sleeping so heavenly
looking into my future.
Growing up day by day,
with my mother side by side,
she'll take care of me day and night,
and defend me with all her love.
Her loving heart and tenderness
will always be with me
no matter what happens.
Her glorious eyes would look out for me,
the day will come
when her eyes would close,
but I won't be sad,
for she'll always be in my heart.
She will never forget me,
and I will never forget her,
her hands will always be wrapped in mine,
trapping all the troubles that come my way.
I know her soul will stand next to me,
wherever I am and whatever I do,
I'll let her move on,
remembering,
she will never forget me,
for I'll always be her loved one.

Bina Tailor (12)
The Swaminarayan School

A Very Special Mum

I can't believe
you were just with me,
left me like a kite, without a string
or someone without control of it.

All those happy times
I spent with you,
and now it seems
my world's complete.

Without you I cannot bear,
then I stare
at the things
you gave me.

I just can't live without you,
I just want to come with you,
I close my eyes to pray to God,
All I see is you in all.

I want to be with you,
now and forever,
within you,
why can't you take me?

Please take me with you,
in all and all,
please forgive me for
what I've done wrong.

Why have you left me in this dark world,
my beloved Mum may God bless your soul.

Premvati Depala (12)
The Swaminarayan School

UNSOLVED, UNCOVERED, UNFOUND

Long ago in a world of silence,
Lay a mystery unsolved, uncovered, unfound.
From the gloomy desert to the vast jungles,
Had this story been told, been heard, been crowned.

Day after day the search went on,
For what was priceless, traceless and clueless.
It's losing its meaning as well as its praise,
For it's the mighty subject on which people made their ways.

Our meaningless thoughts of it being new and great,
May bring destruction, chaos and terror.
For its silence may be the foundation of havoc,
As our pitiful moans will bring us to error.

Its inhabitancy stalls and lurks in our shadows,
For it waits to clobber, crush and claw us.
Its appearance is beyond the control of nature,
As it grins on the first sight of when it saw us.

Days are getting shorter and our life span's decreasing,
Searching for this object of interest in a hurry!
So hear me out and hear me good,
Let it say, and let it be a mystery!

Amar Mandavia (14)
The Swaminarayan School

INGREDIENTS

Throw in some weeds from an overgrown heath,
And some very sharp piranha's teeth,
Some smelly socks with grains of sand,
And top it up with a beggar's hand.

Add some fungi and some leaves,
The smell will reach the top of the eaves,
Some juicy beetles in the dark,
And some rubbish from the local park.

Drop in some deer that are still alive,
Add some ginger cats for nothing survives,
With a patch of baboon's hair,
Now things are starting to flare.

Into this potion to make it sweet,
Add peacock feathers and fresh meat,
Add also lizard's tails,
And why not drop in some fish's scales?

Place an emu's eye,
This should be easy for they can't fly,
Get a jar and smash it open,
Shatter the glass to make sure it's broken.

Now bake this into a crusty pie,
So people who eat it will certainly die,
When you eat it with a crunch,
You know it's really our school lunch.

Jessel Savani (14)
The Swaminarayan School